OUT OF THE RABBIT HOLE

A Road Map to Freedom from OCD

Sheri Bloom & Suzanne Mouton-Odum Ph.D.

Foreword by Fred Penzel, Ph. D.

Due to the personal nature of the following narrative, some names have been changed to respect the identity of the people involved. All names of patients described by Dr. Mouton-Odum have been changed and all identifying information has been appropriately altered to protect the privacy of these individuals.

ISBN: 0615779719
ISBN-13: 9780615779713
Wonderland Press Houston, TX

www.wlpress.com

Dedicated to all who suffer with OCD.

May this book be a reminder of the incredible power that lies within each of us.

TABLE OF CONTENTS:

Foreword

Alice: *"Would you tell me, please, which way I ought to go from here?"*
The Cheshire Cat: *"That depends a good deal on where you want to get to."*
— *Alice's Adventures in Wonderland*, **Lewis Carroll**

"If you limit your actions in life to things that nobody can possibly find fault with, you will not do much!"
— *Alice's Adventures in Wonderland*, **Lewis Carroll**

I once had an OCD patient who didn't show up for his scheduled therapy appointment. I got a call from him the next day, and he informed me he was in the hospital. He went on to explain that he had been hit by a car while crossing the street, had fractured his spine, and was now immobilized in a body cast. "You know, Doc," he said, "I remember what it felt like when the car hit me; I remember what it felt like as my head went through the windshield; and I remember what it felt like as my spine broke. I have to tell you that as bad as all that was, OCD is worse than that."

I think this story says a lot. OCD is a miserable, insidious disorder that has this nasty way of finding out what will particularly torture your mind, and then it proceeds to bombard you with doubtful frightening obsessions about it night and day. It seems to be able to find out exactly what matters most to you, and then tries to take it away. No one knows why it does this. One phrase I constantly hear from sufferers when referring to their thoughts is, "It seems so real." The fear, doubt, and guilt can be so severe that people will destroy their own lives with compulsive behaviors that they believe will relieve these things, but paradoxically only makes them worse. OCD sets your brain on fire, and then gives you gasoline to put it out with. It is hard for most people to appreciate the special agony of OCD and the toll it takes on each sufferer's life.

Sheri Bloom and Suzanne Mouton-Odum have written a very compelling book. Sheri has laid out as good a description of the pain of OCD and working one's way through the tasks of treatment as I have ever read. She is a keen observer of herself and her disorder and her abusive upbringing, with many unflinching observations. She not only shares her successes with readers, she also tells them what it is like to fall down again, brush off the dust, and then pick yourself back up and get on with it. It is a tribute to her that throughout her suffering, she managed to somehow find her way and at the same time, maintain a good sense of herself. She always remained open to learning about herself and her disorder. Not only did she eventually find her recovery, her quest caused her to mature and grow as a person, in the process. The book correctly tells us that the only way out of OCD is to go right through it, and that is exactly where Ms. Bloom takes us in her journey down her *rabbit hole*. Her words ring true and sound exactly like those I have heard from the mouths of many of my own OCD patients, five days a week for the last three decades. She sets a good and realistic example for her readers in terms of what to expect from the all-too-human and imperfect process of recovery.

In the interest of full disclosure, I should mention that Dr. Mouton-Odum and I have been colleagues and friends for over twenty years, so it should come as no surprise that we see eye-to-eye on the many issues concerning OCD. She has always had a keen grasp of what really matters when guiding those with the disorder. While reading her portions of the manuscript, I was struck by how much her words sounded like the very things I tell my own patients. I even found some very useful ideas I intend to borrow and use, myself.

I find the form of this book interesting, as it represents a hybrid of the personal OCD to-hell-and-back narrative combined with an OCD self-help book written by an expert therapist. I have always believed that the messages that books of both types should tell their readers ought to be threefold: 1) You are not alone; 2) There is hope and help for everyone willing to seek it out; 3) The only way out of OCD is to face it and go through it, accepting all that this involves. In my estimation, this book hits all these targets dead on. I have run across many sufferers who believed that they must be the only ones who have problems like these. I have also encountered many patients who struggled throughout their lives not knowing that there were effective remedies, or who slogged through many ineffective treatments and who became convinced that treatment could never help them. Thirty years ago, there were no books on OCD, and there were only a handful of places you could go to for help. As a result, I have always believed that there cannot be too much good information, or too many inspiring stories.

When you set out on a journey into the unknown, it is always best if you can take reliable and knowledgeable guides with you, to point out the correct path, as well as the potential pitfalls. Sheri and Suzanne are well-equipped to be those guides for those willing to take the time to listen and learn. Someone once said that the only thing worse than having OCD, is having OCD alone. With resources such as this, you don't have to feel alone, even if personally, you don't know anyone with OCD. And yet, there are still too many lost sufferers out there with no direction and no one to treat them. There are entire countries with no true OCD experts to turn to for help. Perhaps you will come across this book, and perhaps it will move you to tell yourself, "Enough is enough." And perhaps you will then face those fears and live the life you were meant to live.

Fred Penzel, Ph.D.

Acknowledgements

by Sheri Bloom

My deepest gratitude to Jonathan Zadok. Watching you years ago on television share your experience with OCD opened the door to my own courage. Thanks also for introducing me to the ever-inspiring Dr. Suzanne Mouton-Odum.

Many thanks to Suzanne—you are a co-writer's dream! Your tenacity and conviction, your never-ending faith in our book is a joy to behold. Thank you for sharing this rewarding journey with me.

I will always be grateful to Michelle Beard. Thank you for guiding me up my own Mount Everest. The view is wonderful!

To my *eema*, the woman I met at twenty-six, I give untold thanks and gratitude. Your encouragement that I share my story means the world to me.

Words fail to describe how grateful I am to my husband, my best friend. Thank you for your many loving nudges to remain on course each time I started to slip down the rabbit hole. Without your "tough love," I'd likely still be in Wonderland, following the irrational commands of the Queen of Hearts. And thank you for supporting my dream to help others escape their own rabbit holes.

To our beautiful boys, you are the reason, the fuel behind my desire to help others. This book is about facing your fears—an important reminder for all of us. I love you both always and forever.

A heartfelt thank you to Jeff Bell who inspired me with a new perspective on combating the "Doubting Disease." Thank you for motivating sufferers everywhere to focus on the Greater Good. You, Jeff Bell, are a living example of the Greater Good.

Thank you, Dr. Fred Penzel. Your articles filled with razor-sharp insight have nourished me in times of doubt, motivating me to regularly challenge OCD.

Thank you to Howie Mandel. It takes courage to "come out" with the details of your life with OCD. I admire the humor and candor infused in your words regarding our "Doubting Disease."

Thank you to OCD sufferers and their loved ones everywhere. We are our own unspoken community, and it is because of you that I find the courage to share my journey to recovery.

by Suzanne Mouton-Odum, Ph.D.

Co-authoring this book with Sheri has been an amazing adventure. I could never have written about OCD without the people who influenced me as a psychologist: those who are responsible for teaching me about OCD and how to treat this disabling disorder. Thank you to Melinda Stanley, my early mentor and now close friend. Melinda was the first person to teach me that CBT (Cognitive Behavioral Therapy) is a loving and warm enterprise, not a cold, sterile manualized treatment. Her insight and wisdom helped me to love this work and to make it such a large part of my career path.

Thank you to Charley Mansueto, Fred Penzel, and Ruth Golomb for many late nights discussing interesting cases and how to best help our patients with OCD. They taught me that ERP (Exposure and Response Prevention) is as much art as it is science. In other words, although the process of ERP is always the same, each client is unique in their presentation and treatment is creatively tailored to each individual's specific needs.

A special thanks to Jonathan Zadok who has supported the OCD community in Houston for years and who introduced me to Sheri. Sheri's inspiring story needed to be told and I am honored that she allowed me to help her share it with you.

Thanks to the International Obsessive Compulsive Disorders Foundation (IOCDF) for dedicating so much time, money, and energy to serving people around the world suffering with OCD. For many people, just knowing that their behavior has a name and finding others who have similar fears and behaviors provides tremendous comfort and relief.

Thank you to my family: Brian, Alex, and Hayes for your patience with me while I took time away from our family to write and edit my sections of this book. I have the most supportive family in the world and I could not have done this without you!

Most of all, however, thank you to all of the sufferers with whom I have worked over the years. Facing OCD and trusting a therapist to walk with you through the trenches of treatment requires unbelievable courage. Seeing people get better through repeatedly having the strength to face their fears inspired me to write this book. Your stories have helped me to illustrate the different "flavors" of OCD and I greatly appreciate your willingness to share them.

Finally, thank you to Sheri for facing all of your past demons, and being willing to write your personal history with the hope that it will heal so many people. Writing this book was a risk that you bravely took to improve the lives of countless others. Thank you for trusting me to help you tell your story; it was a pleasure writing with you!

Introduction

by Sheri Bloom

*From the moment I fell down that rabbit hole, I've been told
what I must do and who I must be. I've been shrunk,
stretched, scratched and stuffed into a teapot!*

— *Alice's Adventures in Wonderland,* **Lewis Carroll**

If you are reading this book, chances are either you or a loved
one struggles with obsessive compulsive disorder (OCD). To a
certain extent, all humans are inclined to think and do things in an
effort to reduce the discomfort often associated with a chaotic or
uncontrollable situation. Our human thoughts and behaviors, like
a myriad of other conditions, can be seen on a spectrum. Maybe
you have a lucky deodorant reserved only for special occasions or
avoid walking under ladders to prevent "bad luck." On this end
of the spectrum, your attempts to control undetermined outcomes
are small and not likely considered any cause for concern. As we
move further along the continuum however, those seemingly
innocuous rituals begin to require more and more of our time
and energy, preventing us from living our fullest life. People with
obsessive compulsive disorder engage in repetitive behaviors or

"compulsions" that serve to reduce anxiety which results from intrusive thoughts or "obsessions." Unfortunately, engaging in repetitive compulsions provides both a *temporary* and *false* sense of control over life's unpredictable outcomes.

OCD thoughts (obsessions) can feel like commands that must be obeyed or something terrible might happen. Sometimes that "something terrible" is obvious and specific, while for some people there is a vague sense of "impending doom" that occurs. Listening to the commands of OCD or "giving in" to the relentless demands can lead to impairment in one's functioning; insidiously, a person following the bullying commands of OCD can turn into a slave. At this point, life begins to look a bit like a self-contained prison.

Lewis Carroll's, *Alice's Adventures in Wonderland*, offers a rich analogy for OCD: the infamous rabbit hole. The young protagonist is playing with her cat and spending time with her sister the day she decides to follow a white bunny rabbit into the dark abyss. It is in that very moment, in Alice's decision to chase something outside of herself that the slippery slope begins.

Life with OCD is like a trip down the rabbit hole. OCD is the slippery slope without end, the irrational path filled with commands that—when heeded—only grow louder and are not satisfied...for long. If you recall, it is not until Alice stands up to the life threatening ("Off with his head!") Queen of Hearts that she finally wakes up and makes her way out of the rabbit hole to freedom.

In *Out of the Rabbit Hole: A Road Map to Freedom from OCD*, you will journey through my own personal struggle with magical thinking, irrational logic, and repetitive (yet seemingly necessary) behaviors. Just as Alice is told by some unknown commander to "Drink Me" and "Eat Me," I have been "bullied" into behaviors that, in hindsight, are completely unnecessary. Just as Alice grows more desperate to heed the commands of the Queen of

Hearts, you will read about my futile attempts to appease the bully that is OCD. Ultimately, you will learn about how I, too, faced the Queen of Hearts, fearing for my very life if I refused to obey. It is this refusal to obey, this proactive decision to *sit* with incredible discomfort that catapulted me out of the never-ending rabbit hole of fear and into a world of hard-earned freedom.

On our travels out of the rabbit hole, Dr. Suzanne Mouton-Odum is with us every step of the way. A clinical psychologist specializing in behavior therapy for anxiety disorders since 1995, Suzanne explains what OCD is and how it works. Regarding treatment, she describes what works and doesn't work for challenging and ultimately mastering OCD. Suzanne offers solid techniques for escaping OCD's fear-laden rabbit hole. She also provides prescriptive advice on how to STAY out of the rabbit hole, thereby preventing relapse.

It is important to note Alice might still be in Wonderland— where up is down and day is night— if she never followed her inner compass and stood up to the ever-demanding Queen of Hearts. In doing so, she took quite a risk, as the Queen is infamously known as the moody dictator who repeatedly shouts: "Off with his head!" to many innocent victims. Despite the risk of her own mortality, Alice stood up to the Queen. Each of us has the power to take this risk and climb out of our metaphorical rabbit holes. It is daunting and might even feel impossible, but I hope my journey will only empower you with knowledge and courage. May this book help you map a course to the most delicious destination of all: freedom.

CHAPTER 1
Who Should Read this Book?

I know but one freedom and that is the freedom of the mind.
—Antoine de Saint-Exupery

It was much pleasanter at home ... when one wasn't always growing larger and smaller, and being ordered about by mice and rabbits. I almost wish I hadn't gone down the rabbit-hole—and yet—and yet ...
— *Alice's Adventures in Wonderland,* **Lewis Carroll**

It was the middle of the night, and I was about five years old. I was meant to be fast asleep on my grandparents' makeshift cot in their kitchen; only I couldn't get to sleep. The light on their porch bled between the cracks in the blinds. So I turned the blinds to face the other way. But there was still that blaring light. I turned away from the light and burrowed my head under the covers.

That's when my ears became aware of the inconsistent buzzing of the mosquito zapper on that frighteningly bright porch. *Buzz-buzz ... buzz-buzz ... buzz-buzz.* I could not sleep. My father's much-touted opinion of sleep ping-ponged in my head: if I didn't sleep, bad things would happen. And that's when I began to panic with a flood of unspoken questions. *What would become of me? Would I die? Daddy always said he would die if he didn't get sleep. Was I going to die if I didn't fall asleep soon?*

I began to sweat under the cocoon of my sheets, desperate for cool air but too afraid to contend with the light and mosquito zapping. My heart thudded rapidly in my chest, and a surge of adrenaline shot through my five-year-old veins as I calculated the dwindling hours of sleep left. I repeated the math in my weary but anxious head for hours in a desperate, irrational attempt to salvage the precious time I had left to fall unconscious. It was during this time I became aware of cricket chirps morphing into the early morning sounds of cicadas and crows.

Finally, my hair matted to the back of my neck from hours of anxiety and my young shoulders sore with muscle tension, I drifted off amid a rising sun.

I share that story with you because it has a very happy ending. The little girl filled with enough adrenaline to move mountains was once me. I am grateful to report I am no longer this frightened child. It's a good thirty-two years later, and I am a wonderful sleeper.

But the road from five to thirty-seven was a bumpy, potholed one filled with plenty of sharp turns and blind spots. There were cracks in the pavement, fissures large enough to cause my already unstable foundation to crumble, holes enormous enough to bring me to my knees and literally clawing at the soft earth.

Unfortunately, no one told that little girl she'd experienced an episode of childhood anxiety that would eventually develop into full-blown obsessive compulsive disorder (OCD). No one reached out to give her the help she so desperately needed or let her know there even was help out there. Compounded by a series of stressful life events that taught her the world was unsafe, her anxiety burgeoned. As many of us do when faced with feelings of uncertainty, fear, or "out of control" feelings, we develop handy ways to make these bad feelings go away. These strategies might seem to work, but we can become dependent on them, until we soon feel helpless without them. Before we know it, these relief-inducing strategies bleed into many areas of our lives, seeping into the fabric of our existence. This is OCD.

In the next chapter, you will go on a journey into my cobwebbed past to see how not understanding—or perhaps even ignoring—my anxiety made it fester like a wound covered too long with a bandage. Not dealing with my fears and using these inappropriate, unreliable strategies to manage my anxiety actually made it worse.

In all of my struggles with OCD, in all of my desperate attempts to live a life of freedom from obsessions and compulsions, one of my biggest fears—which filled me with a palpable shame—was the belief I was all alone, isolated from the rest of the world by my fears and behaviors. What I have learned through my journey to recovery is I am not alone; there are over 6 million people in the United States with OCD. Imagine the untold others clandestinely living as I did in silent shame.

I don't want you to suffer needlessly like I did, believing you are alone. Although OCD may feel important and necessary, there is no real reason to suffer with it. You deserve a life of freedom from OCD's insidious demands. *You can master OCD.* It is possible. I did it and continue to do it every day. No, it isn't easy, but it can be done. In the context of this book, you will have the input of Suzanne Mouton-Odum, a cognitive behavioral psychologist who specializes in treating people with OCD, as well as an intimate account of my experience battling, surviving, and facing my OCD head-on. Together, we will walk you through my journey and, we hope, get you started on yours.

A friend of mine recently shared with me, "It's not like I have OCD or something, I just need to put all my bills facing the same way in my wallet." Is this a quirk, or is it more? According to the Mayo Clinic, OCD is defined as, "an Anxiety Disorder characterized by unreasonable thoughts and fears (obsessions) that may lead you to do repetitive behaviors (compulsions)." With OCD, you may realize your obsessions aren't reasonable, and you may try to ignore or stop them. That only increases your distress and anxiety. Ultimately, you feel driven to perform repetitive behaviors or compulsions in an effort to decrease these stressful feelings. To actually be diagnosable, these obsessions and compulsions must cause some significant distress in your life, either with your relationships, work, or daily functioning.

It is common for people to adhere to irrational thoughts and behaviors that, over time, become "superstitions" or "habits." After all, look at all of the superstitious beliefs pervading our world.

1. Stepping on a crack will break your mother's back.
2. Throwing salt over your shoulder will ward off evil. (Watch Rachael Ray do this while cooking.)
3. Spitting after relaying fortunate news prevents the evil eye.
4. Knocking on wood will prevent something from getting "jinxed."
5. Avoiding crossing the path of a black cat.

But there is a fine, insidious line between a couple of innocent rituals and repetitive behaviors that consume an hour or more of your day. There is an invisible but important marker between doing something out of habit and doing something to relieve your anxiety.

For years, I felt alone in my personal struggle with OCD. Without help, I ended up wasting so much time trying to feel in control of things I could not control that it took up a good two hours of each day. Eventually, I was diagnosed with OCD. It wasn't until I got help from a trained professional, one who knew specifically how to treat OCD, that the recovery process could begin.

Whether you are sick of checking to be sure the stove is off or spend more than an hour each day washing your hands or other objects to prevent the spread of germs and disease, this book is for you. Whether you like to have things in your house neatly arranged in an orderly fashion or you can secretly relate to Leonardo DiCaprio's portrayal of Howard Hughes in *The Aviator*, this book is intended for you. Finally, if you engage in behaviors that help reduce your anxiety (washing, counting, tapping, rubbing, saying or not saying certain things, checking to make sure something did or did not occur, repeating actions either overtly or mentally, or doing things in a "certain way"), this book is definitely for you.

Our goal in writing this book is to help relieve the pain and suffering that often come with OCD. Together, Suzanne and I will show you there *is* a way out of the rabbit hole. We all deserve a life of freedom. When you have anxiety, you hold the key to your own prison.

It's time to unlock the door.

The secret of happiness is freedom.
The secret of freedom is courage.

—Thucydides

My name is Suzanne Mouton-Odum, and I am a clinical psychologist. Much of my career has been spent treating people who suffer with anxiety disorders, OCD in particular. I have come to know Sheri through an acquaintance and have been impressed with her ability to cope with the circumstances of her life, not to mention her coping with OCD. We met for lunch one day, just to talk, and the conversation turned into an idea to write a book about OCD. Sheri was finally ready to tell her story, and I wanted to provide the reader with a psychological perspective on both Sheri's OCD specifically and the treatment of OCD in general. Given our respective histories, it was a perfect marriage. Sheri is an accomplished fiction writer (and a beautiful writer at that), and I had recently co-authored a book on trichotillomania (compulsive hair pulling).

While there are several wonderful books published about what it is like to have OCD (*When in Doubt, Make Belief,* by Jeff Bell; *Living with Severe Obsessive Compulsive Disorder*, by Marie Gius) and even more written from a psychological vantage point (*Getting Control: Overcoming Your Obsessions and Compulsions,* by Lee Baer; *Freedom from Obsessive-Compulsive Disorder: A Personalized Recovery Program for Living with Uncertainty,* by Jonathan Grayson; *Obsessive-Compulsive Disorders: A Complete Guide to Getting Well and Staying Well,* by Fred Penzel), there are few that combine the perspectives of both patient and therapist.

My job in this book is to help Sheri describe her journey with OCD by providing the psychological or clinical background to guide readers into the inner workings of OCD and to help explain why people with OCD engage in repetitive, unwanted behaviors.

More important, I hope to explain adequately the rationale for OCD treatment and help readers understand, and be able to recognize, what good OCD treatment looks like.

Sheri has been through Cognitive Behavioral Treatment for OCD, an approach called Exposure and Response Prevention (ERP), and she has been quite successful. Today she lives a full life and is aware of her anxiety and urges to ritualize, but she rarely gives in to them. In this way, Sheri is a perfect person to talk about treatment because she has persevered through it and has effectively mastered her OCD. In addition to describing how she came to develop OCD and what that journey looked like for her, our goal in writing this book is to unravel her story of successful treatment. **People do master their OCD; people do get better.**

Sheri has a history that is quite traumatic and certainly more difficult a childhood experience than most people report. It is even more amazing to me that DESPITE this traumatic history and unfortunate lack of family support, Sheri was able to master her OCD. Even in the best of circumstances, fighting OCD is hard, but given the myriad of barriers that persisted in her life, she is a therapy rock star!

In my practice, one of the first things that new patients ask is: "Is there a cure for OCD?" The truth is **it is not about a cure**. OCD is not like a cancerous tumor that can be surgically removed. Like weight, **OCD must be managed**. People who manage their weight successfully will tell you that once they know what works for them and commit to doing it, it simply becomes part of their daily routine. Some people struggle more than others with weight, just as some people struggle more with OCD and anxiety. Those people who fall into the latter group are going to have to work a lot harder to get their rituals and obsessions under control. One thing I can tell you after treating hundreds of people with OCD is: if you work hard, it **does** get better. After reading

Sheri's story, I hope you will be inspired to challenge your OCD. We can provide the road map out of the rabbit hole, but only you can make the courageous journey. We hope this book helps you decide to take the first step out.

CHAPTER 2
My Story: Down the Rabbit Hole

Life is 10% what happens to you and 90% how you react to it.
—Charles R. Swindoll

*I wonder if I've been changed in the night…was I the same
when I got up this morning? But if I'm not the same,
the next question is 'Who in the world am I?'
Ah, that's the great puzzle.*

— *Alice's Adventures in Wonderland*, **Lewis Carroll**

As I stated in the previous chapter, my road to today has been filled with potholes and caution lights, with gaping fissures and emotional boulders from childhood to adulthood. To understand my journey, I'm now going to introduce you to my family, the people who unfortunately contributed to those figurative bumps in the road. I was raised in a home that was frightening, unpredictable, and, at times, dangerous.

I am sharing this "dark" part of my story for several reasons. First, I think it contributed to how my OCD and anxiety developed. As OCD and anxiety run in my family, it is likely I would have developed these emotional conditions anyway, but the events of my life contributed to the specific form or flavor my OCD took.

Second, I am told most people with OCD and anxiety have pretty normal childhoods, not abusive ones. It's important to note that even with this "dark" past, I was able to gain control of my OCD. So this is really a story of survival and resilience. Again, maybe if I had had a supportive childhood filled with unconditional love, I would have developed a different kind of OCD or maybe I would have had a milder case, but the disorder would have likely reared its evil head. Regardless, I will never know. What I do know is, despite the demons of my past, I not only survived, but thrived and continue to thrive. I hope your reading this book will inspire you to take steps toward facing and challenging your OCD. I am here to tell you: it IS possible!

If you've ever seen Jack Nicholson's performance in *The Shining*, you are already somewhat familiar with my father. Granted, Jack Torrance (the main character in both Stephen King's book and its subsequent film) is a murderer who interacts with ghosts, but both Jack and my father possess volatile personalities and zealously abuse women and children.

Oh how I tried to be a "good girl" for my father. Childhood was peppered with emotional mine-fields, and I worked very hard to avoid stepping on them: exhaustion, hunger, stress, sickness—these were the "real" Jack Torrance triggers in my childhood. So I developed a talent for thinking for him, for predicting his needs before he was even aware of them. If he hadn't eaten lunch, I knew to bring him food; when he was upset about something at the office, it was my job to make him laugh; when he kicked our dog, I made sure to be hiding in my bedroom closet until his fury passed.

But my father is a child abuser and there is no rhyme or reason to when or why abusers attack. Like anxiety, attempting to control an abuser by always trying to be one step ahead is both ineffective and exhausting. In my case, I believe staying one step ahead of his emotions actually set the stage for my OCD to blossom. I was an expert at "following the rules" and "performing the rituals" that made life easier and less stressful whenever possible.

Case in point: It was a day or so before Christmas when my older sister woke me before sunrise. Apparently, there was a treasure trove of toys waiting to be wrapped in our garage. I remember peeking inside the chilly room and eyeing enough presents to make my five-year-old heart soar with delight.

Too late, we heard my father's screams behind us. My body was yanked over Jack's thighs as he repeatedly yelled profanities and bellowed what would become his angry mantra to all three of his children: "May you rot in hell!" All this as his belt strap slapped my buttocks until it hurt to sit.

In my young mind, I deserved what my father did. Of course I never should have looked at those presents. Those gifts were *his* surprise to his children and now I'd just ruined the surprise for everyone!

Hours later, when my buttocks were still too sore to sit down, my father apologized to me. There were tears in his eyes as he explained he'd punished the wrong daughter: My older sister was a "sneaky bitch" who tattle-tailed on me. He hugged me and said I was his "Sheri love"—a name he used when he wasn't busy threatening my life. He told me I was his favorite daughter.

I was always my father's favorite—until I took his candy bar; borrowed his pen; didn't make him laugh; didn't stay away from him when he was tired or sick; didn't agree with whatever he said. Then I was "the bitch," "rotting in hell," "dead" to him and someone he was going to "cut up in little pieces." Years later, whenever the "voice" of OCD gained volume, it was often my father screaming in my head; in time I learned it was impossible to pacify OCD and Jack Torrance. So I stopped trying. Self-preservation and freedom lie in not listening to or paying attention to that voice. Turning the volume down on those fearful (albeit irrational) thoughts actually weakens them, allowing them less traction in our minds.

Whether genetic or spiritual, there is an invisible umbilical cord that ties children to their parents. In rare cases, we need to sever them. But I didn't know that at five, ten or even twenty years old. So I did the abusive tango with my father, bending over backwards to be daddy's good little girl, desperate for him to love and accept me.

The world is a dangerous place to live in; not because of the people who are evil, but because of the people who don't do anything about it.

—Albert Einstein

My mother is a perennially overweight woman who sees the world through morbid lenses. I suppose this is a by-product of living forty-three years with Jack Torrance. And while my father never physically abused her as he did his three daughters, he did wallop our sad-eyed mother with plenty of verbal insults. She was "slow," "fat," and often described as a "pig," "elephant" or "Buddha" (referring to her large belly) by her spouse. She typically brushed off his insults, but sometimes, often late at night, his angry rants would leave actual tears in her depressed eyes.

During these nightly screams (accompanied by several door slams and pounding feet), my sisters would huddle together in one of their bedrooms. But feeling that invisible umbilical cord connecting me to my mother, I felt a pull to head into her bedroom and comfort her.

Insidiously, my role of daughter morphed into the part of mother and therapist to the weeping woman in the bedroom. Our conversations typically went like this:

Mother: That's it. I've had it with him. I'm going to leave that sick bastard. He can't treat me like this.

Door slamming; screaming threats can be heard in the background.

Me: We can go anywhere you want, as long as we're together.

Mother: I'm not long for this world, honey. I probably won't make it past forty.

Me: Oh mom, don't say that. I couldn't live without you. I wouldn't want to live without you. I'd rather not live than lose you.

Mother: (with a spark in her eyes and a slight smile) Don't say that, honey. That's not right.

Of course, when my sisters and I were being physically abused or verbally threatened, my mother had very different responses:

"I didn't hear him say anything bad."

"You're too sensitive. Don't take everything your father says personally."

"You need to apologize to your father. You know how he gets when he's hungry/tired/sick/stressed."

Bottom line: my mother enabled the abuse and was therefore just as lethal to her children's well being. But, as with my father, I didn't know cutting off ties was an option. So I spent years trying, in vain, to win her affection and bring happiness to those sad eyes; I spent years trying to conceal my thin figure in hopes she'd stop insulting my "all bones" body; I spent years trying to love her so she might one day love me back. In the face of my father's regular outbursts of violence, I perceived my mother as a veritable angel for staying with her husband. I dangerously elevated my mother to the role of saint and grand protector of my life. From my pre-adolescent perspective, it became like breath to worship the woman who had to contend with the volatile monster each day. When Jack Torrance used the strap on me for grabbing his Snickers bar or called me the "C" word because I interrupted his television show, by contrast, my mother was suddenly launched into this celestial creature, my safe harbor, my everything.

There are pictures of me from childhood, a stick-figure of a little girl clinging to her mother for dear life. It is painful to see these pictures, the neediness of my young self almost palpable. If my mother is aware of her daughter's tight hold, she doesn't show it in the photos. In almost every photo she looks defeated, ready to leave the world she inhabits. Years later, as a grown woman, when I think about those pictures, I see a child trying to grab (in vain) a false lifeboat—my mother, who was the source of a great deal of doubt for me. Just like OCD, I believed if I did X, Y, and Z, my mother would love me and fill me with self-assurance. It would be many years before I learned strength and empowerment come from within.

Life whispers in your soul and speaks to your heart. Sometimes, when you don't have the time to listen…Life throws a brick at your head.

—Author Unknown

By the time puberty hit, I'd put my hopes for a loving relationship with my parents on the backburner. A steady fuel of anger, frustration and loneliness remained unarticulated after years of emotional and physical abuse. It was the background noise of my psyche—no different than the chatter we tune out in a crowded restaurant. I'd become an expert at tuning out my feelings and denying the ever-increasing anxiety flooding my veins.

I was the poster-child for low self-esteem. My parents' message was ingrained in me loud and clear: I didn't matter. Our thoughts create our reality. I believed I didn't matter and yet craved love and affection—a perfect recipe for anxiety, a perfect recipe for trouble. Instead of dealing with the irrational notion that I didn't matter; instead of accepting my parents as toxic; instead of listening to my own voice, my anxiety sky-rocketed and self-esteem plummeted to new depths.

Boys, boys, boys—they were a temporary fix for my self-esteem. It didn't matter if I liked a boy or not. I hungered for *their* attention, *their* approval of me. It is no surprise I met a young man with an equally dysfunctional family as mine. When he told me his mother once chased him around the house with a knife because he did poorly on a test, I mentally pushed away the red flag. In the very beginning of our relationship, it didn't matter that he shaved his entire head after he learned I'd been out on a date with another boy. I was too busy feeling ecstatic that Jon *liked me*, that he cared enough to do something so extreme for me. As with my parents, I'd developed a talent for denying the truth of things, for denying my own thoughts and feelings, for denying the obvious red flags waving in my face.

Jon lied that he quit smoking; Jon blinked when he got nervous; Jon had mood swings I couldn't keep up with; Jon cried a good deal and disappeared for long periods of time only to re-emerge romantic and charming. His volatile nature seemed almost natural to me after years of emotional abuse from my parents. And like my parents, Jon needed help. Maybe I couldn't fix my parents, but there was hope I could nurture and heal Jon. So I offered myself up as his maternal and romantic savior.

There was a sense of comfort I found in caring for Jon. Finally, there was someone who loved me, who needed me, who valued me. And when my father called me the "C" word in front of Jon, he became *my* protector and savior. Jon promised once we were married, he'd never let my father speak to me that way again. Jon and I were the perfect dysfunctional couple. Together, neither one of us felt the need to deal with our destructive pasts as we role-played the give-and-take of love we never received. Unfortunately, when we don't deal with our issues, they only get bigger.

One sunny fall day, I came home to our apartment to find my troubled new husband hanging in our hallway. My mother was with me, but I'd managed to push her out of the way so she wouldn't see Jon. She drove me to the doctor while I screamed uncontrollably.

"Stop it already! Quiet!" my mother said.

Only I couldn't. It was the first time I could remember disobeying MOM. Between my screams I could hear the doctor reprimanding her.

"She needs to let it out," he said.

The doctor's words were a light in a dark prison. *Yes! Yes!* — a part of me screamed inside and out.

And yet I felt an overwhelming sense of responsibility for Jon's suicide. In my mind, I was both the judge and the criminal, and my broken psyche charged me with guilt for not saving Jon. It is no surprise the trauma and guilt from Jon's death opened the floodgates of OCD for me. For months, I was haunted by the obsessive visual memory of Jon's body, and I found myself doing any and all rituals possible to feel psychologically back in control. Of course, as Dr. Fred Penzel wisely writes, "If you want to think about it less, think about it more." Unfortunately, I didn't know that at the time, so my anxiety and those violent images only grew.

A week after Jon's suicide, I went to my first therapist meeting ever. My father interrupted the session to inform me that he didn't have all day. He told me I was selfish, and that the world didn't revolve around me just because I was a widow. My mother agreed.

My parents' mantra became, "You need to move on" within days after Jon's funeral. I wanted to cry and scream but there was no safe place to go. Despite my desperate need to grieve, I felt an even stronger need to please my parents. So I buried my pain and returned to work full-time within a week of Jon's passing.

I'd been in such a hurry to go down the aisle, to get away from my parents, to run from their message that "I didn't matter." And where had it gotten me? Back home with the very toxic people I was desperate to avoid.

My anxiety grew worse as I continued to believe my parents' advice. A frequent question plagued my mind: What the hell is wrong with me? Instead of allowing myself the time I needed to mourn, I regularly reprimanded myself for not *moving on* and *getting over it*. I immediately began working fifty plus hour weeks; my childhood fears of the night and of not being able to sleep worsened; I began dating within months; I made certain my calendar was ridiculously full and never went near the bed until I was close to collapsing. I avoided my feelings altogether by staying busy, distracting myself with mundane activity, and not allowing a second of time to consider what I was feeling inside. I became even more disconnected from my intuition and emotional reality.

Fear is conquered by action.
When we challenge our fears, we defeat them.
When we grapple with our difficulties, they lose their hold upon us.
When we dare to face the things which scare us,
we open the door to freedom.

—Author Unknown

My father regularly told me I couldn't "make it" without them. When he told me to "drop dead" at bedtime, by morning he told me I was beautiful and could be a movie star. Whenever I'd feel a surge of anger over my mother's neglect and lack of protection and affection, she'd give me a weak pat on the back and say, "Oh honey," and I'd melt.

According to Princeton University, "Stockholm Syndrome is a term used to describe a paradoxical psychological phenomenon wherein hostages express adulation and have positive feelings towards their captors…essentially mistaking a lack of abuse from their captors as an act of kindness." The victim or captor typically views her oppressor as giving life simply by not taking it. In a nutshell, the victim learns to take crumbs from the perpetrator and sees those crumbs as jewels.

My Dr. Jekyll and Mr. Hyde father never let me forget that food, shelter and clothing existed because he provided these things (ignoring the fact he was typically unemployed and we lived off of my mother's salary.) Without his actions, I'd have nothing. Without my mother's advice and wisdom, I'd be lost. Without them, I would die.

But Jon's death forced me to take stock of my life. When you are snuggling in bed with your husband one minute and seeing him hanging from a blood-spattered noose the next, you are forced to re-evaluate your life.

The first few nights after Jon's death, I slept with my mother. Despite her coldness and insistence I move on, I felt that invisible umbilical cord pulling me towards her for comfort and irrational safety. My evening anxiety was at an all-time high and never once did it cross my mind to give myself permission to feel this way—which of course only made the anxiety fester.

Unfortunately, Jack Torrance stormed into the bedroom on the third night. "Go back to your own bed! This is my bed. A man sleeps with his wife. You are a grown woman. You should be ashamed of yourself. It's not normal to still be sleeping with your mother."

As terrified and confused as I was, I knew I needed to move out of my parents' home and get my own place. It didn't matter that every time I closed my eyes I saw my dead husband; it didn't matter that I barely slept and couldn't eat meat without thinking of corpses;

it didn't matter that I'd developed a ritual of checking closets, locks, windows and behind doors to make sure I was safe. Deep down, I knew it was time to leave the choppy waters of home and try, despite my parents' message to the contrary, to make it on my own.

The little girl you met at the start of this book grew up in an abusive home. Fear and doubt were her constant companions. One could argue that, in time, performing rituals and compulsions offered that child a sense (albeit, a false one) of control, that it became an unconscious, psychological crutch. But let me be clear and state: **OCD and abuse do not go hand in hand.** Children who are abused grow up to be adults without OCD; likewise, you can have OCD and come from a loving home. Clearly, I had a genetic predisposition to the disorder.

I want you to know that I am not writing from some ivory tower. I am disclosing my journey through the psychological rubble and physical pain that ultimately led out of the rabbit hole to a life of freedom, inner peace, and happiness. After a childhood and young adulthood of trauma, I still managed to face, battle, and ultimately dominate the beast of OCD. My hope is that reading my story will inspire you to fight your OCD. I know what it's like to be in the emotional clutches of OCD; I also know it is worth the effort, the internal fight, to gain a life of freedom outside of OCD's constant tyranny.

Our greatest power is the power to choose. We can decide
where we are, what we do, and what we think. No one can take the
power to choose away from us. It is ours alone. We can do
what we want to do. We can be who we want to be.

—Author Unknown

Sheri's story is not the common OCD story. Not everyone with OCD has endured physical and emotional abuse and certainly not the traumatic suicide of a loved one. However, her childhood experiences did contribute to the development of her OCD in a unique way. During Sheri's early development she learned to anticipate, as best she could, her father's moods and actions; she found ways to avoid his anger; and, ultimately, she attempted to skirt away from his abusive behavior. She performed actions to pacify him, to avoid danger and possible physical harm. She developed a great skill for anticipating his mood, and preventing any negative outcome. In a way, she was trying to control his mood and, thus, her safety. Unfortunately, her "control" over him was both temporary and ineffective. It never permanently stopped him from abusing her because there was always something else for him to become upset about. These attempts to avoid and control her father's behavior are strikingly similar to how OCD works and, ultimately, may have contributed to the development of Sheri's OCD.

The common thread is the desire to control situations that feel very out of control. It is never a foregone conclusion that abuse and trauma lead to OCD; they do not. However, like most other people with OCD, Sheri found successful ways to temporarily control her environment when it felt (and was) out of control. In my practice, I see people who have, for the most part, had very good childhood experiences. Many of my clients have tremendous family support and nurturing relationships, but they are still plagued with obsessions and compulsions. While Sheri's story is more extreme in nature, I believe her recovery from OCD, given her traumatic experience, is what makes her story so remarkable and so beautiful.

Gambling: The sure way of getting nothing for something.
—Wilson Mizner

OCD is A Losing Bet—Every time

A client recently gave me a brilliant description of what life with OCD is like: Having OCD is like walking into a casino with $1,000,000.00 in my pocket. While approaching the craps table I am told by a very reliable source if I put my money on red, I have 99.99% probability of winning, whereas if I put my money on black there is only a .01% chance of winning. Knowing that the "sure" bet is to put my money on red, I choose black "just in case," every time. I choose black simply because there is a very remote chance I might win. It makes no sense, but I do it every time!

With OCD, he *knows* he is putting his energy into the lowest possible probability "bet"; he *knows* he will most likely lose, but he makes that bet every day, hundreds of times. Although people with OCD are not betting with money, they are betting with their time and energy. Where do you put your time and energy? Do you put your time and energy into the most likely outcome or the least? Are you engaging in activities intended to prevent something bad from happening that, odds are, is very unlikely to happen?

Ultimately we know deeply that the other side of every fear is a freedom.
—Marilyn Ferguson

Who is in control: You or Your OCD?

OCD is about control. As you will read in the next chapter, OCD develops into what seems like a lifesaving flotation device, but in actuality is a pair of cement shoes. Before launching into the next chapter, I want to make a point about control. Rituals are actions performed with the goal of reducing anxiety about something "bad" happening. In this way, a person feels in control of the bad outcome. Ask yourself this: What are you really controlling by doing your rituals? Think of the woman who has to have her bills all facing the same direction in her wallet. Perhaps she does this because she believes if she does not, her children will not be safe. Is she truly controlling the safety of her children or is she controlling her *anxiety* about the safety of her children? The obvious answer (or maybe not so obvious to some) is she is only controlling her anxiety. Unfortunately, this anxiety management tool is pretty faulty, because inevitably the anxiety will return and yet another ritual must be performed. She will spend the rest of her life having to keep those bills facing the same direction. She has become a slave to anxiety management.

The Nature of Negative Reinforcement

Most of us have heard of positive reinforcement: when a positive is given which increases the likelihood of a behavior to occur. An example of this would be a parent who gives a reward for his child going potty on the toilet. He "learned" that using the toilet leads to "good" things, thus the behavior is reinforced. Most of us are also familiar with punishment: a negative event makes a behavior less likely to happen. An example of this would be getting a speeding ticket. Theoretically, the "punishment" of having to pay a fine results in reduced speeding behavior.

A phenomenon less talked about but which is highly reinforcing is called "negative reinforcement." Negative reinforcement is when a negative is removed and thus produces a positive result. An example of this would be if you have a headache and take some pain reliever and the headache goes away. The negative (headache) is removed and you feel better (very reinforcing).

The concept of negative reinforcement is what happens with OCD. You feel anxiety (very uncomfortable) and then perform a ritual, which reduces the anxiety, thus you learn the ritual is very important in anxiety reduction. For example, the woman who feels compelled to put her bills all facing the same way in her wallet is doing so to reduce her anxiety (negative reinforcement). Whether or not the ritual has anything to do with the safety of her children, it nevertheless causes a desired reduction in her anxiety, which means it is highly reinforcing. I think this is important to understand because it explains how OCD ultimately works. The ritual does serve a temporary function (to reduce anxiety), yet has very little to do with actually changing the ultimate outcome of the situation (keeping children safe). The association between bills facing the same way and children being safe is arbitrary and meaningless, unless you are the person Sheri described earlier. For her, the association is compelling and quite meaningful because it helps her to feel less anxious about her children. It lets her relax. Begin to think about your behaviors and the associations that you make between your rituals and your anxiety. Begin to question whether or not your rituals are really effecting any change over the "feared" outcome. Are they?

Read the directions and directly you will be directed in the right direction.
— *Alice's Adventures in Wonderland,* **Lewis Carroll**

So what can you do when the pull to perform a ritual metaphorically taps you on the back? As you will learn in this book, do the opposite! In the case of the woman who feels the urge to put her bills facing the same way in her wallet, I'd suggest she purposely put them in random order. LOTS OF ANXIETY WILL FOLLOW, but interestingly, her children remain safe. Why is this? Because the bills don't have anything to do with the safety of her children in the first place! That belief was all an illogical creation of her mind. That belief gave her comfort and relief, resulting in a false sense of security about her children's welfare.

As you read the next chapter, consider your behaviors and what you think they control versus the reality of what they actually control. Ask yourself: Are you or your fears in control?

CHAPTER 3
Creating a False Lifeboat: OCD

It takes all the running you can do to keep in the same place.
— *Alice's Adventures in Wonderland*, **Lewis Carroll**

I was twenty-five and living in my own New York apartment. Despite the occasional doctors' visits where I circled the freshly acquired title of WIDOW, and the ever-dwindling looks of unabashed pity from colleagues, life seemed almost eerily back to normal within months after Jon's death. I was working a good fifty to sixty hours a week; I was exercising regularly, eating balanced meals, and dating again; I spoke positively, sounding like a walking Hallmark card to friends and family: *"I take each day as it comes. Life is a gift. This too shall pass. There is so much good in my life; I just focus on life's many blessings."*

Cue the barf bags.

Friends marveled at how well I was doing. My parents' annoyance with my early tears seemed to diminish. Everyone was pleased with the young woman who appeared healthy and content. And oh how much I wanted to please. So this "healed," "happy" Sheri was the person I showed to the world every day.

But inside I was in hell. Inside I was dying right along with Jon. Inside were unrelenting questions without tangible answers: *Where do we go when we die? Does Jon blame me for his suicide? Can Jon see me? Does Jon hate me? Is there something that I could have/ should have done to save him?*

No one knew, no one could have guessed the confident woman I *played* during the day returned to her apartment each night, terrified. No one saw that empowered woman's heart race as she watched her home insidiously transform into a cavernous, dangerous playing field where inexplicable violence was waiting behind every door, underneath the bed and on the other side of the shower curtain.

As going to therapy or getting psychological help of any kind is frowned upon, if not derided, within my biological family, I didn't let myself even consider getting professional help. So instead I devoured self-help books which typically only made me feel worse. Self-help books can be wonderful tools for all kinds of recovery, but they can also be potent medication and I was mixing way too many figurative drugs. The books only confused me more and this further increased my sense of failure and the anxiety that went with it. I needed a book about OCD and behavioral treatment. When you have a throat infection, you don't take an antacid; when you are struggling with OCD, a book on positive self-talk won't really help much.

With no one to turn to and lost in a sea of ever-increasing turbulent waters, my mind needed something it could hang on to for dear life. My nightly routine of checking and ritualizing became my lifeboat. The unspoken fear I was somehow responsible for Jon's suicide manifested in an hour-long routine filled with magical thinking and compulsions to confirm each night I was *definitely, without a doubt,* alone and safe in my apartment. I feared I hadn't been nurturing and loving enough to Jon and, now that Jon was on the "other side," he was going to "get" me somehow. And so my fear bloomed and suddenly God was angry with me, too, egregiously disappointed in me for not paying more attention to Jon's pain, for not getting my husband the help he had so desperately needed. My nightly routine looked something like this:

The sky is still light as I close the apartment door. I check to see that it's locked. There is an immediate sense of relief upon checking the front door is locked. But once I turn around to face the looming stairs above me, my heart is racing. Jon hanged himself right near stairs that look too similar to the ones in this new apartment. But no, there's no one here. Release. Wait—I need to check no one is in the coat closet, the bedroom closet, the kitchen pantry, behind the shower curtain, the closet in the hallway. Whew—release.

I talk to friends, eat dinner and take a shower. The sky is now the color of coal. My heart begins to race again. There is that pull to check everything again: behind all the doors, behind the shower curtain and there's a new pull to check beneath the bed now. Whew! It's time to go to bed.

In bed I must pray to God ritualistically. The words need to be said in an exact order and clearly pronounced. If the words are messed up in any way or it just doesn't feel right, e.g., if I feel a "pull" to fix the prayer, I must start again from the beginning. This prayer routine could last anywhere from five minutes to a half hour—depending on my level of anxiety that day.

Finally, (big sigh), I feel "allowed" to go to bed. Once I am in a cozy place in bed however, the pull, the bully whispers to me: "You better check that front door. You wouldn't want someone to come in during the night and hurt you." So I check, ashamed at each step I make down those stairs. On my way up, I notice shadows on the wall. A thought pops into my head: "That could be Jon in that dark corner. Maybe he isn't dead after all. Maybe he made it look like he committed suicide, but he's still here on earth waiting for you when you least expect it."

I am exhausted and want nothing more than to sleep, but the bully is telling me I can get my sleep if I just check behind the doors and the shower curtain and this time, too, look inside the oven just in case there's something horrifically frightening waiting in there for me.

Eventually, I would get too tired to listen to the bully and would pass out after enough rounds of checking. Sometimes my night-time routine lasted an hour, sometimes two. It filled me with shame, which, of course, only made the bully stronger and more demanding.

If you would have told that twenty-five year old woman, "You have OCD, honey," she would have given you a dirty look and shook her head until it fell off. She may have even laughed in your face, one of those big guffaws with a lot of hot (and fearful) air behind it.

Today, I have a wonderful cognitive behavioral therapist, who tells me the average person struggling with OCD waits about seven years before getting help. Most often this is because many lack the knowledge about treatment for OCD or they cannot find a therapist who is adequately trained to treat OCD. I'm one of those average people. I want better for you.

You see, by keeping my OCD a "dirty little secret," the disorder mushroomed out of control. The very rituals and compulsions, meant to give a physiological release and provide a sense of control amid chaos, grew like those Gremlins (*Gremlins*, 1984) audiences are warned not to feed after midnight.

For me, OCD is nothing but a big bully. Sure, he might sound all-powerful and omnipotent, but he's all smoke and mirrors. The truth is OCD personified is nothing more than an old, helpless, overweight guy who's more scared than you! He's the voice who whispers to you to check the stove is off and when you do it, he asks, much more boldly, "*Are you sure the stove's off? And while you're at it, you better check that oven. You wouldn't want to cause a fire, would you?*" He's the martini an alcoholic craves. He's the invisible pull that gets my feet out of a warm bed on a cold night only to check (for the fifth time) the front door is most definitely, positively, absolutely locked. He is the voice of my father, promising me I will be safe once I do A, B and C; only once I do this, I learn I need to do the rest of the alphabet—two more times just to make sure!

You are what you are and where you are because of what has gone into your mind. You can change what you are and where you are by changing what goes into your mind.

—Zig Ziglar

Call it a pull, a bully—call it the invisible puppeteer—it doesn't matter. What matters is that you identify the entity that is OCD as something *separate from the true you, the authentic you.* OCD is simply a misfiring in your brain. For years I listened to and obeyed the voice and this only made the parasite that is OCD grow stronger. When you engage with OCD, when you believe the only way to feel better is to respond like a slave to OCD's every command, then you are nothing more than a prisoner in your own soul. **OCD is a liar**. It is nothing more than faulty wiring in your brain that announces there's danger when there isn't any. It's only when I began to perceive OCD as a foreign parasite or a crazy tyrant that I could begin to ignore it and, more importantly, *challenge* it.

Failure is not fatal, but failure to change might be.
—**John Wooden**

Viewing the Lifeboat as a Mirage

The title of this chapter could not be more apropos: *Creating a False Lifeboat*. The truth is, although it *feels* like a lifesaving tool, OCD is only capable of providing superficial and temporary relief. Although OCD thoughts (obsessions) are technically a part of you, they are not a helpful part and you can learn not to heed them. You must know OCD for what it is: a **false** lifeboat. I think the main reason OCD feels so vitally important to people is it reduces unwanted anxiety (negative reinforcement). This *feels* good. This *feels* helpful. Unfortunately, those feelings won't last because OCD is incredibly effective at reducing anxiety for the present (sometimes only for a minute or two). **The relief OCD may provide is only temporary** and is, ultimately, fuel for the proverbial OCD fire. OCD feeds on your fear and your rituals. Every time you do a ritual, OCD gets fed, and therefore it gets stronger. Every time you resist doing a ritual, OCD gets starved, making it weaker.

The goal is to starve your OCD until it has absolutely no power over you. Although it feels good to perform rituals to reduce your OCD, although part of you may even believe your OCD is somehow helping you, it is not.

OCD is only a mirage, not a true lifeboat. A true lifeboat would provide support, safety and lasting reduction of your anxiety, but this is not the case. The relief OCD provides is short-lived and manipulative. Once you begin to view OCD as a negative, not a source of refuge or comfort, you can begin to work.

OCD: The Annoying Bully

So how do you begin to think of OCD as a negative influence in your life? Sometimes it is helpful to think of OCD as outside of yourself, as a "bully." Imagine your OCD was a separate person, a roommate, who followed you around all day and told you what to do, e.g., "Don't touch that, you better wash," "Still not good enough, better wash again." "You probably ran over that person; you better go back and check." "You probably, secretly, want to kill your loved one; you had better stay away from the knife drawer," etc. How would you feel about this person? Would you listen? Would you do what he said? Would you kick him out? For some people, it is helpful to begin to think of their OCD as separate from themselves, because the truth is, it is not reflective of the true you.

Other people with OCD prefer to recognize OCD as a part of themselves, just as alcoholism or Attention Deficit Disorder is, but with the help of calculated and informed therapeutic intervention, OCD can be managed. Whether you view OCD as a part of you or as a separate entity, OCD is a problem if it interferes with your ability to function in life. Does it keep you from doing things you need to do? Does it take up a lot of time in your life? Does it prevent you from enjoying otherwise enjoyable things?

Obsessions are False Alarms

Some OCD researchers have described obsessions as false alarms. When a fire alarm goes off, people become a little nervous, wondering if there is a fire, and they follow all of the directions promptly to get to safety. If, however, the fire alarm goes off and it is announced as merely a drill, people still go through the motions of exiting the building; they are still able to hear the alarm, but they no longer have anxiety about a fire. OCD is basically a false alarm in your head. You may still hear the alarming thoughts telling you that there is danger present, and they may stay for an extended period of time, but you can learn to register there is no danger. In a way, these unwanted and frightening thoughts can become "background noise" in your head; something that is there but bearing a negligible impact on you. Whether you choose to view OCD as "outside" of you, like a bully, or as a part of you that signals a "false alarm," it doesn't really matter. The important point to understand is these thoughts are neither true nor helpful. Obsessions, fears, and images all signal danger when there is no danger. They request action to be performed to reduce feelings of danger when no action is needed. It is this increase in fear/anxiety leading to action to reduce the fear/anxiety that is the insidious OCD cycle.

Thoughts are not Real

Because a thought exists inside our head, we sometimes give it more power than if it was a person outside of us. An important fact to remember is **thoughts are not real**. They are passing and fleeting events which mean nothing unless we give them meaning or energy. It is common for people to *believe* thoughts are important simply because they are thoughts. However, this is patently untrue. I can have a variety of thoughts that are not only untrue, but ridiculous. For example, I can think, "my hair is purple" or "I want to kill my husband," neither of which is remotely true.

Learning to watch thoughts and, eventually ignore them, is an important part of beating OCD. Do you have thoughts that may not be true? Can you think a thought that is purely ridiculous? Can you acknowledge some thoughts are pure imagination?

> *If I had a world of my own, everything would be nonsense.*
> *Nothing would be what it is, because everything would be*
> *what it isn't. And contrary wise, what is, it wouldn't be.*
> *And what it wouldn't be, it would. You see?*
>
> — *Alice's Adventures in Wonderland*, **Lewis Carroll**

The Nature of Obsessions

OCD is fascinating with respect to the fears or obsessions that get selected as they are, oftentimes, the most abhorrent thoughts a particular person could possibly imagine. Whether it is the loving mother who suddenly fears she will lose control and harm her child, or the devoutly religious man who becomes fearful that he secretly has a pact with the devil, the process seems to be the same. Most often, OCD selects the thing that scares us the most. OCD is analogous to the "boggart" in J.K. Rowling's third Harry Potter book, *The Prisoner of Azkaban*. The "boggart" presents itself as the object a person most fears. Now, I realize knowing this does not make OCD any less scary. However, by understanding the process, you are better able to understand why OCD manifests in the way it does. It is **not** that you want or desire the feared thing to happen; it is precisely because **this is the most horrific thing imaginable** to you that it presents in this way. In Rowling's novel, the charm that will defeat the boggart, "Riddikulus," is said as the wizard thinks about the feared object in a funny way, e.g., a giant spider wearing roller skates or the scary Professor Snape dressed as a woman wearing makeup. Simply thinking about the feared creature as "funny" or "ridiculous" weakens it. This is not far off from what we teach in OCD treatment. We teach people to face their fears and to perceive them in a different way, one that is less frightening. In doing this, one can weaken the thought. In Rowling's book, Harry and his friends are terrified to face their fears, but after a few tries, they see the boggart is really harmless, and they begin to have fun with the "Riddikulus," charm. OCD treatment can be very daunting at first and overwhelmingly frightening for some, but as treatment progresses, it becomes easier and much less scary.

OCD as the Fisherman and You are the Fish

OCD is relentless in its pursuit of you! Think of OCD as a fisherman, and you are the fish. You are in the water, looking at the worm dangling from the fisherman's hook. Are you going to bite? Are you going to give into the temptation to listen to your OCD, to give into the rituals? If you do, guess what? You are now officially hooked! Once you bite that hook, (and taste the savory worm for only a millisecond), you are involved in a brutal struggle for what seems like your life. No matter how much you struggle, OCD has you at every turn; it slowly and painfully reels you in, leaving you exhausted and hopeless. If you think of OCD in this way, your job then is to sit and watch the worm on the hook, AND NOT BITE! When obsessions are tempting you, just recognize them for what they are: thoughts. You can see them out there and not react at all, (not bite). You can learn to acknowledge to yourself that these thoughts exist and sometimes tempt you, but you do not have to give them any energy at all.

Learning to Swim- Abandoning the Lifeboat

Whether you think about your OCD as a bully, a false alarm, a boggart or a fisherman, it is important to understand that the process you must go through is the same. This book will teach you how to ignore or not respond to obsessions. The point is **not to engage** with your OCD. **This is hard**, especially when performing rituals seems to effectively reduce your anxiety, right? Wrong! Remember: your anxiety might get better for a moment, but it always comes back, often worse than before. That taste of relief is like the fish tasting the worm: it tastes pretty good at the moment, but that good taste comes with a huge cost. In reading this book, you will learn to ignore or "not bite" the worm. In psychology, we call this "response prevention." Response prevention means **not doing** the thing(s) that OCD tells you to do. In time, you will also create "exposures," which means engaging in and eventually seeking out the things that trigger your anxiety, e.g., touching an object that you believe might be contaminated with some unpleasant germs or contaminants. By doing this, you will learn to fight your OCD, and you will learn to swim!

CHAPTER 4
From the Frying Pan into the Fire: The Stealthy Nature of OCD

I know who I WAS when I got up this morning, but I think I must have been changed several times since then.

— *Alice's Adventures in Wonderland,* **Lewis Carroll**

When you attempt to eliminate risk from your life, you eliminate, along with it, your ability to function.

—**Fred Penzel**

A good year after Jon's passing, I met Max. Max was independent, consistent, emotionally stable and confident. Our courtship occurred once I was living on my own—without the irrational and dangerous influence of my parents. After experiencing the horrific tragedy with Jon, maybe I knew more than the average twenty-something about what I wanted in a partner, or more accurately, what I didn't want. It was no surprise that I found Max's even temper, honesty, and nurturing yet independent nature, attractive. By my late twenties, Max and I married. One year later, I was pregnant with our first child.

But while my more mature self knew what was best for me in a partner, my OCD still thrived in the background. My habit of checking and ritualizing had somewhat diminished with the aid of Max sleeping beside me each night. Max loved me despite my quirky habits of OCD, but I hid, as much as I could, the extent of my irrational fears and behaviors from him. Irrationally, I'd reasoned that Max was "protecting" me from Jon's ghost. It was only when Max had a business trip that the familiar pull would begin to stir, a yanking from some shameful place inside of me to check and ritualize. Only now I wasn't living in a one bedroom apartment. Now my home consisted of a two story townhouse with three bedrooms and two and half baths; now there was a front AND back door needing to be checked to ensure they were securely, definitely locked. And God forbid Max left a window open before he left for the airport; I now needed to check every window was shut tight and locked as well. There was the oven; there was the stove; there was a laundry room with a questionably long and dark cabinet. I learned to hate and fear Max's business trips; I learned to hate and mistrust myself for behaving like a crazy woman each time his car pulled out of our garage.

It is human nature to avoid frightening and unpleasant experiences. I didn't want to be a terrified and ashamed woman pacing the halls for two plus hours a day with a growing baby inside of me. So I did what I'd become an expert in: pretending to be okay, while lying to myself and everyone around me. I called my close friend, Jessica (who ironically was later diagnosed with OCD) and invited her to sleep over on those nights when Max was traveling. I told her that I missed Max so much and would love the company.

I wish I could tell you that by the time I was a newly married woman with her first child on the way, I knew I had OCD. But the truth is I had no clue. Jessica had shared her ritual of saying certain prayers in the shower to protect the people she loved. It didn't matter if she was already scrubbed clean and remained in the shower long after the hot water stopped running; she felt compelled to linger there, soaping herself up with the irrational logic that her shower prayers would protect her family and prevent misfortune from happening. I felt sorry for her, never once making the connection that I too suffered from the same, disabling disorder with merely a different flavor. Then one night, halfway through my pregnancy, I woke up and walked into the bathroom and made up this rule, this irrational, inexplicable rule: *If you want to get back to sleep, whatever you do, don't look at yourself in the mirror.*

Huh? Where did *this* pull come from?

Instead of questioning or challenging the thought, I adhered to it. How I wanted to look at my burgeoning belly and admire my changing body. But if I even snuck a glance at myself–oh the anxiety, oh the *pull* to walk into the bathroom all over again and go through the motions (washing hands, putting on lotion), but this time make certain *not* to see myself at all. Insidiously, I had planted a new ritual, and unknowingly, strengthened my OCD. Without help or guidance to stop adding new compulsions and with an ever-growing shame at what I ignorantly considered my insanity, OCD quickly festered until I was prisoner to countless time-consuming, self-imposed rules.

You cannot teach a man anything;
you can only help him find it within himself.
—Galileo Galilei

Cutting the Umbilical Cord

Within two days after our first child was born, my mother began insisting my father babysit. By this point, I still shared a co-dependent relationship with my mother, and only saw my father as the abuser, the "bad guy" in my biological family's dysfunctional history. Our dialogue, one of our last ones, went something like this:

Me: I'm afraid Dad will abuse the baby.

Mother: Oh please! Your father didn't abuse you girls until you were much older.

Her corrosive logic was apparent to me—more so with the backdrop of new parenthood and a sudden, mama-bear like hunger I felt to protect our son. My decision was final: my father would not be permitted time alone with our child.

I was thirty years old when I stood up to my mother and father for the first time in my life. There was an adrenaline that came with saying no, an adrenaline not altogether different from resisting a compulsion. And just like with OCD, the bully (my mother and father) got louder and made me question my decision not to give in (handing our son over to his disturbed grandfather). My father proceeded to get on the phone and threaten Max's life. In his equally illogical world, Max was the reason I was not being a "good daughter" and letting him babysit his grandson. I listened on the other extension to his familiar threat: "I'm going to cut you up into little pieces." Only this time, the threat was to my best friend, my husband.

With Max, my emotional rock by my side, I felt empowered not to be swayed by my father's disturbing threats. And then there came the final blow, the kind that comes close to an out of body experience:

Mother: Your father and I are a united front. If you want me, you must accept your father, too.

Me: No. I refuse to let him be with our son without Max or myself there.

Mother: Then give the baby a kiss for me and have a nice life. CLICK.

I remember listening to the dial tone until the recorded voice came on the fractured line. The invisible umbilical cord had been officially severed with my first attempt to object to and defy my parents. Yet instead of feeling empowered and free, I felt sick with anxiety. All I could hear was my father's steady mantra throughout the years: *You can't make it without us–especially without your mother.*

It would be several months before my mother tried to contact me. As a result, I barely slept and my anxiety spiked to new heights. As a new mother—suddenly and unnaturally bereft of a co-dependent, emotionally volatile relationship with my own mother—I felt even more lost and afraid than I did after Jon's suicide. Not surprisingly, the pull to control things grew right along with my unprecedented fear.

Now my days were filled with intruding, obsessive thoughts about needing to blink and swallow and incredibly morbid, intrusive images of people I loved being nothing more than skeletons. Without the bullying voices of my mother and father, I felt lost and lacking an identity for the first time in my life. So my mind became its own bully. I could no longer look at my husband, our baby, myself or anyone without seeing horrific images of us as covered in a frail veneer of flesh and blood that would erode to nothing but a pile of bones shortly after death. Looking back, my macabre thoughts made sense: with my dysfunctional, dependent relationship suddenly severed, I was unexpectedly catapulted both emotionally and spiritually out of control. All of my life, my opinions and beliefs came from my parents' sick mantras. And now, at the age of thirty, I was without their commands and the twisted logic they had ingrained in me. If I "couldn't make it" without them, I was nothing more than a skeleton, flesh and bones rotting away with my suddenly upturned psyche.

Or maybe there was a much simpler explanation for my sudden obsession with skeletons: perhaps my mind was trying to distract me from thinking of the heart-wrenching pain I was experiencing. After one particularly challenging night filled with compulsions and rituals, I called an emergency help line. The "angel on earth," the nurse whom I spoke with for a good hour, helped me understand the why behind my intrusive thoughts:

"Your parents abused you, and until now, this is all you've known. Your body may be that of a grown woman, but your mind is overwhelmed by this sudden freedom. And so your thoughts, everything you see and hear is that of a child," the nurse said.

That nurse, that "angel on earth," helped me understand that the sudden cutting off of my parents had left me hyper-aware, ultra-cognizant of everything from our eyeballs to the beating of the human heart. I was not all together different from a slave who, after years of brainwashing and abuse, finds herself suddenly free. Freedom is often, as in my case, a scary, uncertain beast. The end of any unhealthy and dependent relationship comes with potential side-effects; one of mine was the burgeoning of OCD.

Despite Max's insistence to the contrary, I believed I was slowly going insane. I began taking Ambien, a prescription sleeping pill, because it blurred some of the intrusive images; it allowed me to skip some of the rituals I otherwise felt compelled to do. Ambien allowed me to relax so I could function during the day. Ironically, I loved the way the drug forced me to lose control. Ambien numbed the pain surrounding my parents and kept frightening thoughts at a fuzzy distance: what if my parents are right? What if I can't make it without them? What if I contributed to Jon's suicide and my sick parents' behavior? What if I didn't try hard enough to make the relationship with my parents work? What if my father was right, that I will die without them?

In hindsight, it was those fearful questions that were at the root of my compulsions. I attempted to relieve the anxiety produced by these thoughts by performing more and more rituals to reduce these terrible feelings. I became a slave to the tyrant of OCD. I was exhausted and becoming hopeless. Why did other people not have to do these things? Did I know something they did not or was I privy to knowledge they did not have? Nevertheless, I was confused, emotionally spent and scared to death about what the future held for me and for my family.

My intrusive thoughts, rituals and checking morphing out of control (there's that irony again), I grew desperate for help. I made an appointment with a psychiatrist. I told him about my parents and my recent dependency on Ambien. I told him about my intrusive thoughts, purposely neglecting to share the rituals and compulsions I was too embarrassed to admit. BIG MISTAKE! How can we expect our doctors to help us if we aren't forthcoming? Had I been honest, I could have gotten help for my OCD much sooner. The longer a person waits to get help for OCD, the more entrenched their behavior becomes, and as a result, the more challenging it can be to conquer it.

The doctor gave me a prescription for Lexapro and told me I had anxiety. I read online about people taking Lexapro and, as is typical with many people suffering with OCD, fearfully noted the side effects. A flood of frightful questions began circulating my over-stimulated mind: *What if the medication doesn't work? What if I feel worse? What if it makes me go crazy? What if it makes me unable to sleep?* Refusing to consider the many good potential responses to the medication, I refused to take the anti-depressant.

It wasn't until I read an article in *Oprah* about a journalist who developed an irrational fear of her teeth falling out, and the rituals she developed to prevent this feared outcome, that a light bulb went off in my head. The writer went on to describe her obsessive, intrusive thoughts, as well as her elaborate and time-consuming rituals. She described how a cognitive behavioral therapist helped her to overcome her OCD. Suddenly there was hope for me; suddenly there was a name for what I had! And what was even better: I wasn't slowly going insane; I was suffering from a **treatable** disorder!

Maybe it was staring at a painting in our bedroom, waiting all night until the sky grew frighteningly light for it to fall down that made me respond to that *Oprah* article; maybe it was making sure my wallet was snapped shut until my thumb was sore; maybe it was reciting a prayer card until the words blurred in my head that finally led me to the realization I had OCD. Maybe I was finally ready to accept I had a problem that I was not able to manage on my own. Regardless, the important point I want to make is that recovery from OCD cannot begin until we **acknowledge the disorder**. As long as you remain in denial, OCD holds all the power. OCD likes to remain hidden, a dirty little secret that grows best in stealth, in private.

It's time to bring OCD into the light so that you can see it for what it is: nothing more than shadows.

We are only as sick as our darkest secrets.
—Walter Cubberly

When the disease is known it is half cured.
—Erasmus Colloquies

A Psychological Perspective

So what is OCD officially? By definition, OCD is defined by the American Psychiatric Association's Diagnostic and Statistical Manual for Mental Disorders- 4th Edition (DSM-IV-TR) as:

A. Either obsessions or compulsions:
Obsessions are defined by (1), (2), (3), and (4):

1. Recurrent and persistent thoughts, impulses, or images that are experienced, at some time during the disturbance, as intrusive and inappropriate and that cause marked anxiety or distress.
2. The thoughts, impulses, or images are not simply excessive worries about real-life problems.
3. The person attempts to ignore or suppress such thoughts, impulses, or images, or to neutralize them with some other thought or action.
4. The person recognizes that the obsessive thoughts, impulses, or images are a product of his or her own mind.

Compulsions are defined by (1) and (2):

1. Repetitive behaviors (e.g., hand washing, ordering, checking) or mental acts (e.g., praying, counting, repeating words silently) that the person feels driven to perform in response to an obsession or according to rules that must be applied rigidly.
2. The behaviors or mental acts are aimed at preventing or reducing distress or preventing some dreaded event or situation; however, these behaviors or mental acts either are not connected in a realistic way with what they are designed to neutralize or are clearly excessive.

B. At some point during the course of the disorder, the person has recognized that the obsessions or compulsions are excessive or unreasonable. Note: This does not apply to children.

C. The obsessions or compulsions cause marked distress, are time consuming (take more than 1 hour a day), or significantly interfere with the person's normal routine, occupational (or academic) functioning, or usual activities or relationships.

D. If another Axis I disorder is present, the content of the obsessions or compulsions is not restricted to it.

E. **The disturbance is not due to the direct physiological effects of a substance (e.g., a drug of abuse, a medication) or a general medical condition. (APA, 1994)**

Examples of common obsessions include worrying about contamination, inadvertently or purposefully causing harm to someone else, and doubting whether you locked the door or turned the oven off. Obsessions are difficult to stop, and many people typically respond with anxiety and attempts to make the thought go away. Obsessions are generally upsetting and tend to interfere with daily functioning.

Examples of compulsions include such behaviors as hand washing, checking, repeating, confessing, seeking reassurance and counting. Compulsions may take on ritualistic aspects when they must be performed in a certain way. Compulsions or rituals work to decrease anxiety. These rituals tend to be frequent and feel as if they are necessary. If a person with OCD is unable to perform a ritual or is able to resist doing a ritual, her anxiety tends to temporarily worsen.

Most people with OCD have both obsessions and compulsions. For example, some people have a germ contamination obsession. These worries can be about specific germs (e.g., flu) or about bodily fluids or contaminants (blood, urine, semen, radon, asbestos, etc.) in general. In addition, the concerns about germs can be directed at either avoiding germs to prevent harm to themselves (catching a disease), or to prevent harm to other people by spreading the germs (inadvertently spreading a disease or contaminant). People learn quickly that by washing their hands or objects (cell phone, remote control), they can reduce these fears, thereby reducing their anxiety quite effectively. Hand washing then becomes a ritual (or compulsion) that is performed when anxiety is present.

The obsession/compulsion cycle is very powerful. Even more important, **the compulsions that people perform actually make their obsessions stronger**. After a hand washing ritual, a person tends to feel better because she no longer has the contamination obsession. However, this relief is only temporary, because the obsession is likely to return. So, what will happen next? Well, she has *learned* that, last time, washing hands made that obsession "go away." In other words, *learning* has taken place: "The last time I felt bothered by germs, I washed my hands, and felt better. So, I'm going to wash my hands again..." And so begins the cycle.

Who has OCD?

Approximately 2% of the population or 6 million people in the United States currently have obsessive compulsive disorder (OCD). OCD is the fourth most common psychiatric disorder. In other words, OCD is a problem many people deal with. You are not alone. OCD is a disorder that affects people from all walks of life. Symptoms may start during childhood (between the ages of 10 and 12), while other people begin developing symptoms around the age of 19 years.

The International Obsessive Compulsive Disorder Foundation (IOCDF-www.ocfoundation.org) is a wonderful organization dedicated to education and outreach for people suffering with OCD around the globe. If you have not heard of the IOCDF, I recommend that you visit their website and, if possible, attend a conference to meet other people like you and learn, from world experts, about the treatment for OCD. As with other psychological disorders, feeling isolated and alone can intensify the experience and may lead to feelings of sadness and hopelessness.

Why Do I Have OCD?

There is nothing that you "did" to develop OCD. It's not your fault. Research shows that many people with OCD have someone else in their family who also suffers with this disorder. If no one in your family has OCD, there may be a higher likelihood that someone in your family suffers from another anxiety disorder such as panic disorder or generalized anxiety disorder. During your development at some point, you may have had an experience which "taught" you that a compulsion or ritual would reduce your anxiety. This learning experience can be very subtle, like accidently performing a behavior and noticing that it reduces your anxiety, or quite overt, like seeing a TV show informing you that there is e-coli bacteria in red meat, and it can harm you. A person with a predisposition for OCD might watch this program and then begin to avoid touching and/or eating red meat. Researchers are not 100% sure why a person develops OCD, but believe there is likely an inherited component, particularly in OCD that develops in childhood.

OCD is a neuropsychiatric disorder, meaning that it exists due to the functioning of your brain. Brain scans have shown that the brains of people with OCD behave differently than the brains of people who do not have OCD. During this "learning" experience of OCD, your brain begins to form pathways that are different than those of a person without OCD. Additionally, **researchers have documented the change in brain function following cognitive behavioral therapy for OCD. This means that you can actually change these pathways in your brain by "teaching" your brain other ways to think!** This is probably the most important finding in the history of OCD research. More on treatment in the next chapter, but for now, know that although OCD is not "curable" it is "correctable."

OCD tends to be a gradually-developing disorder. However, some cases develop very quickly, without warning and particularly after a powerful learning experience. In Sheri's case, her OCD developed very rapidly, after witnessing her first husband's suicide. She was likely predisposed to developing an anxiety disorder due to her childhood fear of not being able to sleep, and this childhood fear probably gave her OCD its flavor. Thus, Sheri was more likely to develop OCD than someone without a history of anxiety.

Some people develop OCD after having contracted an illness such as a strep infection or Lyme Disease. In these cases, the resulting OCD is called "PANDAS," short for "Pediatric Autoimmune Neuropsychiatric Disorder Associated with Streptococcus" or "PANS" when the cause is thought to be an infection other than strep. Symptoms of OCD can manifest suddenly, following an infection, or current symptoms can become much worse during or after an infection. It is believed that in these cases, the OCD symptoms are the result of the body's reaction to the infection, not to the infection itself. For these children, evaluation by a physician to determine whether or not a strep infection is present, and treatment with appropriate medications can be the first step. Regardless of the etiology of OCD (PANDAS, PANS, genetics or learning experiences), OCD is treatable with behavior therapy. It takes a willing and committed participant, but change is possible.

It's Complicated

OCD can interfere so much in a person's life that it actually leads to having other types of anxiety and/or depression. It is not uncommon for people with OCD to develop depression as a result of living with near constant fear and anxiety. For people who have OCD and another disorder, addressing their OCD may be the first step in decreasing the non-OCD issues. Therefore, treatment focusing on the OCD could decrease these other symptoms.

There is also the case where OCD exists among several other, more pressing concerns. Examples of this might be if there is a developmental disorder such as autism or Asperger's Syndrome, or if a person also suffers from bipolar disorder or is suicidal. In the case of a person experiencing suicidal thoughts, it is always important to first make sure that the individual is treated for depression successfully, before proceeding to work on OCD. Depression and OCD commonly occur together, especially if the OCD has been present and disabling for some time. Having OCD can cause a person to feel hopeless about the future, to not enjoy the present, and to ultimately give up. If any of these describe you, it is important to contact a therapist who has knowledge about the treatment of OCD. Feeling hopeless is a hallmark of depression and **there is hope for people with OCD**. Taking steps toward recovery, as Sheri did, opens the door to empowerment and ultimately freedom from the chains of OCD.

Complications are present when a person fears that she will do something out of control to hurt herself (like hurl herself over a ledge or jump into oncoming traffic). Such fearful thoughts are not to be confused with suicidal thoughts. If a person **fears** doing these things and does **not** want to do them, but is afraid that they might lose control and do them, it is OCD "talking", not suicidal thoughts. Presentations such as this can be confusing and take the expertise of a trained therapist to tease out what is what. In any case, sometimes OCD is not the disorder that needs to be addressed first, but can be worked on after other, more pressing concerns have been resolved.

When OCD is Severe

For some people, OCD becomes so severe that they are not able to function in their daily lives. Individuals can spend hours each day ritualizing, causing interference in work, family and/or social functioning. For individuals with severe OCD, interventions such as medication, intensive outpatient treatment, or inpatient hospitalization are often necessary to help get them begin to establish new behaviors and beliefs. Sometimes, fears are too great to be addressed in outpatient therapy sessions, and more intensive intervention is required. If OCD takes up more than one hour a day, it is worthy of treatment with a trained therapist. If you are not able to function in your daily life (work, family or social), it is worth talking to a therapist about more intensive treatment.

Understanding Your Obsessions

OCD is an umbrella term describing patterns of behavior involving recurrent, intrusive thoughts, images or fears followed by repetitive, unwanted behaviors that serve to reduce these negative events. Despite the common obsessive compulsive process, the disorder manifests quite differently across people, depending on their particular fears. Traditionally, OCD has been described based upon a person's ritual, e.g. washing, checking, confessing or counting, etc. However, recent discussions have moved toward understanding OCD as having dimensions or themes. Rather than looking at the *ritual* to understand the OCD, Martin Franklin, Ph.D. a colleague and OCD specialist, refers to these dimensions as "obsessional themes." The following is a list that describes most, if not all, of the OCD-themed fears or concerns (obsessions):

- Fear of unwanted harm to self
- Fear of unwanted harm to others
- Contamination fears (these can involve concerns about harm to either self, other, or both)
- Unwanted/intrusive sexual thoughts, images
- Superstitious thoughts, fears

- Unreasonable somatic (health) concerns
- Morality/Scrupulosity fears (Fear of being an amoral or bad person, not being truthful, or of blasphemy)
- Not just right feelings (Where a person has the need to perform or repeat an action until it feels "right." This can involve checking, counting, ordering/arranging, tapping, evening up, rubbing, etc).

To help you identify some of your obsessional themes, ask yourself:

- What do I think would happen if I did not do these rituals or compulsions?
- What am I afraid of?
- What is the thing that I most fear will happen?
- What bad thing am I trying to prevent?
- If this bad thing did happen, what would it mean about me?

Most people with OCD have one or more specific fears or obsessional themes. For some people, their obsessions fit into more than one category. This is okay. I recently saw a woman in therapy who feared getting HIV from kissing another person. This fear falls into the "fear of harm to self" as well as the "contamination" theme areas. For obsessions such as this, it is not important to identify exactly which theme it falls into, but understand that it can fit into several.

There is a segment of people with OCD who have primarily rituals, with no specific fears (obsessions). These people fall into the "not just right" category or what has come to be known as Tourettic OCD (TOCD). Folks with "not just right" OCD or TOCD do not have specific fears; they just don't feel right until things are a certain way. For example, a person may not feel right touching the arm of a chair with her right hand alone; she would feel compelled to then touch the chair with her left hand to "even up." Another example is of a person who has to turn the lights on and off until it "feels done." This is different from doubting yourself about having turned off the lights; it is the result of an internal feeling of "things do not feel just right."

This "not feeling right" form of OCD can present itself in many ways. People with this type of OCD describe more of a physical sensation or discomfort than simple anxiety associated with fear. Sometimes people do perform tics in response to obsessions with the intent of reducing anxiety. This is also considered TOCD, even though it is a tic being performed, rather than a ritual. The important thing to remember about "not just right" OCD is that there is oftentimes no specific fear driving the rituals; the rituals are driven by feelings of physical discomfort that are relieved by the ritual.

Primarily Obsessional OCD

Another type of OCD is the Primarily Obsessional OCD. With this type of OCD, a person experiences fears without overt rituals. An example might be a man who fears that he may violently harm his newborn child. The thoughts of harming his child are quite disturbing, and he tries repeatedly to push them out of his mind. Although rationally he knows that he loves his child, he questions his love merely because he *has* these thoughts. In response to these unwanted thoughts, he begins to avoid certain activities, such as bathing the child (to avoid drowning her), holding the child when standing near a balcony or ledge (to avoid hurling the child over the edge), or chopping vegetables in the presence of the child (to prevent himself from stabbing her to death).

Further, he may also have mental rituals, such as saying things repeatedly to himself or in a certain way to "prove" he wouldn't do these terrible acts. If you were to view this man for a day, you would conclude that he does not have OCD, because he does not engage in any observable rituals. This conclusion would be incorrect though, because his rituals are subtle, internal and not obvious to the world. Just because these rituals are subtle, internal and not readily observable does not mean, however, that they are not disruptive to him.

What Are Your Rituals?

As described earlier, rituals or compulsions are the behaviors you perform to reduce your anxiety or discomfort. They can cross over all of the obsessional themes. For example, checking behaviors are common across the fear of harm to self (e.g., check to make sure that I didn't send an email with an error in it), fear of harm to others (e.g., drive back to check to make sure I didn't run over someone), unwanted sexual thoughts (e.g., check to make sure I did not sexually assault a person), and unreasonable somatic (health) concerns (e.g., check to make sure I don't have any unusual bumps or spots on me) to name a few. It is important to know what your rituals and compulsions are in order to help you understand yourself and your behavior.

Ask yourself:
- What are the things I do to reduce my anxiety produced by my intrusive thoughts and fears?
- What behaviors do I engage in regularly to reduce my fear(s)?
- What do I do to make myself feel better?

_____

_____

_____

_____

Common compulsions or rituals are: washing, checking, avoiding (avoidance touching certain things, going certain places, etc.), repeating, doing something in a particular way, following a "rule," asking for reassurance, counting, ordering/arranging, and saving. A ritual is anything you feel you "must do" in order to reduce your bad feelings.

Habits are at first cobwebs, then cables.

—Spanish Proverb

In my work with many people who have OCD, I have seen some common, underlying driving forces that contribute to increases in OCD behavior. Two common triggers for the onset of or increase in existing OCD are events that cause a person to feel "out of control" and/or events that mandate increased responsibility. In Sheri's case, she experienced a series of events that were very out of control (her abusive father, her first husband's suicide, her parents' rejection of her after she stood up for herself), and tremendous increased responsibility (getting married, severing the relationship with her parents and having a child). In response to these life changes, she responded in ways which helped her feel "in control." While she had a childhood history of subtle OCD or anxious behaviors, her OCD burgeoned as these stressors increased.

It is important to understand, while OCD behavior *feels* like it is giving you control over your anxiety and bad feelings, in essence, it is very out of control. The control you feel is not only superficial but, ironically, it creates internal chaos, rendering you out of control. People believe their rituals are helping them control some aspect of their lives: health, safety of self, safety of others, prevention of bad things from happening, or a need to know for sure that something is right. The truth is, in all of these cases, there is still risk. It is impossible to control any of these things. Rituals only provide a quick, but short-lived, reduction in anxiety. The recommended approach for mastering OCD is to learn to tolerate and eventually ignore these worries/fears, so that the compulsions are no longer necessary.

When in Doubt: SIT!

Although at first it may sound ridiculous or downright painful to "sit with" your anxiety by not engaging in your rituals, this is the treatment of choice for OCD. Expert Guidelines for Treatment of OCD include a specific cognitive behavioral approach called Exposure and Response Prevention (ERP). In ERP treatment, a person is asked to create a hierarchy of fears (from least to greatest) from which to work. During treatment, the client, with the assistance of a therapist, works on facing her fears (*exposure*) by starting with those at the bottom, (the smaller fears), and eventually, working up to the larger and larger ones. The person is asked to feel the feeling of fear, and to stick with it while facing the fear. In other words, they are asked NOT to do the ritual that usually reduces their anxiety. This NOT doing of the ritual is called *response prevention*. Over a period of time (usually about forty minutes), the feeling subsides. In this way, the person learns that rituals do not have to be performed to reduce fear; the feeling will reduce on its own. This process of reduction in anxiety is called *habituation*.

Let's take the example of Bill, who fears getting cancer and checks his body excessively for changes, spots, bumps, etc. He might search on the Internet for information about certain types of cancer, spend hours a day in front of the mirror, and will likely visit with his doctor to address the things which cause him concern. His life might become very focused on reading about cancer, checking or scanning repeatedly in the mirror, looking for bodily changes, and making doctor visits (sometimes to the ER). Each time he performs a check and visits the doctor, his anxiety is reduced, and he is relieved to learn his "bump" is nothing to worry about. However, before long there is another "bump" or "spot" that causes concern. His anxiety shoots up and he finds himself back in the doctor's office seeking reassurance that he is okay. Bottom line: **OCD does not work in the long term**.

Figure 1 depicts the process of anxiety escalation and reduction that occurs with the use of compulsive or ritualistic behavior. This reduction in anxiety is rapid and therefore very reinforcing, followed by the reductions in anxiety rituals bring. The spike represents the obsession(s) and the dramatic dip represents the reduced anxiety after a compulsion. Interestingly, anxiety does not stay down for long, but starts to creep up again, oftentimes to new heights.

Figure 1

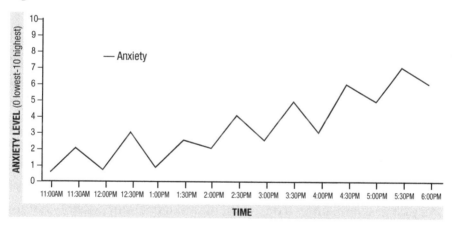

If Bill were to engage in ERP treatment for OCD, he might be asked to say to himself statements like "I might have cancer," (lower on his hierarchy), and then imagine having cancer (higher), and going to a hospital where people are being treated for cancer (higher), and *not* be allowed to check, investigate, inquire with doctors, have tests performed or research symptoms about cancer. Bill saying, "I might have cancer" and imagining that he is diagnosed with cancer is the exposure on his fear hierarchy. The "not checking" is the **response prevention,** and it refers to the **not doing** of the rituals that have previously brought relief.

When Bill initially allows himself to think the thought "I might have cancer," his anxiety will spike very intensely. To be successful in treatment, Bill's task is to sit with this thought and allow it to be there. He must also sit with his anxiety and allow it to be there as well. This is *very hard* at first. People with OCD are quite accustomed to making the anxiety *go away*, not sitting with it and letting it be there. It is common for people doing exposure work to think thoughts that will reduce their anxiety in that moment. For example, an anxiety-reducing thought might be "I am just kidding. I don't really think that I have cancer." It is important to be aware of these thoughts because they can interfere with the exposure work and can cause therapy to fail. During exposure, anxiety typically starts to subside after about forty minutes (habituation).

Later in treatment, some cognitive behavioral therapists may ask him to write a script about his being diagnosed with cancer, going through treatment and, eventually, dying from cancer (highest on his hierarchy). Turning toward the feared stimulus (possibly having cancer) is referred to as **exposure**. Bill is exposing himself to the thing he most fears, thus elevating his anxiety in a step-by-step fashion, going from least anxiety-provoking to most anxiety-provoking. This script might then be read into a recorder and he might listen to it every day, several times a day, until his anxiety about possibly having cancer abates. As stated earlier, this process of anxiety-reduction in response to repeated exposure is called **habituation**. Although this may seem extreme, **it works!** If a person can "habituate" to a tape recording about his dying from cancer, seeing a small spot on his arm becomes much less scary. Again, this therapeutic intervention is referred to as Exposure and Response Prevention (ERP) and has been proven in research studies to reduce OCD effectively.

Figure 2 depicts this therapeutic process. Instead of engaging in the ritual which leads to abrupt anxiety reduction, Bill does not engage in behaviors to reduce his anxiety or he says and does things that actually increase his anxiety. The resultant anxiety eventually abates causing him to "learn":

1. He can tolerate his anxiety, and eventually his anxiety will reduce on its own,
2. With practice, his anxiety becomes less and less in response to this particular fear and
3. Not engaging in these compulsions *does not* lead to his having cancer.

Figure 2

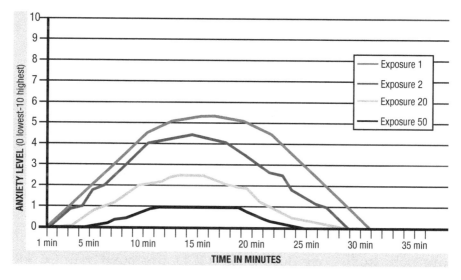

OCD: The Doubting Disease

OCD has long been referred to as the "Doubting Disease." People with OCD want to know "without a doubt" that:
"I don't have cancer."

"My kids are safe."

"I am safe."

"I do not have dangerous germs in my world."

"Bad things are not going to happen to me or those I love."

The problem is we can never know anything *without a doubt*. Herein lies the OCD problem. **Doubt is everywhere.** Part of the solution to overcoming OCD is allowing doubt to exist and eventually becoming okay with it.

Below is a list of more meaningful and beneficial statements for some common OCD fears:

"I do not have any evidence I have cancer."

"I am reasonably sure my kids are safe."

"I wash my hands before I eat, so I am less likely to ingest dangerous germs."

"Bad things will happen to all of us, unfortunately, but I will cope with them as best I can when they do."

Sounds impossible, right? Accepting doubt is one of the cornerstones to successful treatment, but it does not come easily. In the chapter on treatment for OCD, you will learn about behavioral changes that ultimately lead to changes in beliefs. Right now you may not believe that you could ever think this way, but it is possible. Interestingly, the most successful avenue to changing one's beliefs is changing one's behavior, which is precisely how ERP works. In addition, the many scientific research studies conducted on OCD treatment tell us **ERP works better than medication alone and better than supportive therapy** (traditional talk therapy). As stated earlier in this chapter, brain scans before and after ERP show actual changes in brain functioning in people with OCD. Oftentimes, the best treatment is a combination of medication and ERP.

Although this book is not a treatment manual and is not intended to replace ERP, it will give you an overview of the rationale and approach a good OCD therapist will take. After reading this book, you will be well-informed about what good treatment looks like and what to expect from your therapist. We hope this perspective will give you the confidence to move forward, and seek treatment with a professional trained in ERP.

A Word on Medication

Anti-depressant medications are a viable treatment for OCD. Medications have been found to reduce OCD. For people who respond to medication treatment, their symptoms reduce between forty to sixty percent. In fact, the treatment of choice for OCD involves both CBT and medication. Sometimes medication can help reduce fears and obsessions, making the process of exposure and response prevention less overwhelming. Other times, medications help to reduce depression that can be secondary to OCD. It is worth discussing medication use with your therapist and psychiatrist or physician to determine if you are a candidate for a trial of anti-depressants. For some people, it is their OCD that prevents them from trying medications. Obsessive, irrational beliefs about medications possibly causing harm can lead to refusal to try them. Again, challenging fears and irrational beliefs leads to new information that can ultimately dispel these beliefs and lead to wellness.

CHAPTER 5
Getting to Work: Learning to Defy the Queen of Hearts

It is impossible to get out of a problem by using the same kind of thinking that it took to get into it.

—Albert Einstein

It's all her fancy: she [Queen of Hearts] never executes nobody, you know.

— *Alice's Adventures in Wonderland,* **Lewis Carroll**

I was giddy with relief after I made my first appointment to see a Cognitive Behavioral Therapist. In my naïve eyes, Dr. Morgan Powers was going to treat me for this annoying and shameful "thing" known as OCD. Going to her office would be akin to removing some warts or a handful of bunions: the process might be unpleasant, but in a few sessions, my anomaly would be a distant memory.

Morgan quickly corrected my assumption. After asking a series of questions with oftentimes embarrassing answers, she diagnosed me with obsessive compulsive disorder. She clarified OCD was highly *treatable,* but she couldn't guarantee it would ever go away.

No guarantee? *Gulp.*

She shook her head and compared OCD to Russell Crowe's character in *A Beautiful Mind.* Based on the life of theoretical mathematician, John Forbes Nash, Jr. (Crowe), the story depicts his struggles with schizophrenia. The schizophrenia manifests itself with several imaginary individuals (hallucinations) who fight for Nash's attention. By the end of the film, Nash learns to accept the hallucinations, yet simultaneously disengage from them and, as a result, gets his life back.

Morgan's point was loud and clear: like Nash, I may always hear the OCD voice, pulling me to ritualize or check things, but with work and time, the voice would grow quieter and less annoying. Although OCD and schizophrenia are very different disorders, they both can involve intrusive thoughts, beliefs or images that, with practice, can be ignored. As they are ignored, they lose their ability to control the sufferer.

I didn't like Morgan's answer one bit. I wanted reassurance that OCD would be gone forever. I wanted it extracted from my psyche like a bad wisdom tooth. I didn't like gray—I wanted black or white. I wanted certainty.

"Yes, that's another sign of OCD: wanting a definite yes or no. You need to get comfortable with uncertainty."

And with that, she handed me the first session's homework assignment.

Security is mostly a superstition. It does not exist in nature....
Avoiding danger in the long run is no safer than outright exposure.
Life is either daring adventure or nothing.

—Helen Keller

The OCD Hierarchy

My first assignment was to make a list of the things that scared me (obsessions) in order of their scariness from least to most scary. Next, I was to write down next to the fear, what I did to make the fear go away (compulsion). While I was still upset and angry (with an intangible sense of claustrophobia thrown in the mix) at the idea that OCD was chronic, looming far greater was a sense of desperation. I was psychologically drowning, a prisoner of my own psyche. I didn't have the luxury of debating the accuracy of Morgan's assertion that OCD was a lifelong condition. So I got to work.

Even taking the time to sit down and merely write down my obsessions was a daunting, heart-racing task in itself. At first I just jotted down the scary thoughts (obsessions) and subsequent actions (rituals) which came to mind. By the time I was finished, I'd filled up three pages.

It was sobering and eye-opening to consider the long list in my lap. The familiar flood of shame and fear washed through me, but something new emerged along with it: anger. How *dare* I waste my life doing these ridiculously unnecessary checks and rituals! Life is so short and here I was, throwing away a good hour and a half each day (two plus hours if my husband was out of town) worrying about things none of us has control over! Anger is a wonderful motivator for change. Anger weakens and has the potential to destroy fear.

Fuming, and with a determination I'd never felt before, I listed my obsessions and compulsions in hierarchal order from least to greatest. Here's a significantly condensed snapshot of what my list looked like:

1. Might have left the lights on downstairs, and might be up all night if this is a possibility- Make sure all lights are off downstairs.
2. Might have left the bedroom door unlocked, and might be up all night if this is a possibility- Check to make sure that the front door to bedroom is locked.
3. Might have left my purse on its side, and might be up all night if this is a possibility- Check that my purse is sitting upright.
4. Might have left my purse open, and might be up all night if this is a possibility- Check that my purse is closed.
5. Might have left my wallet open (again—feared insomnia)- Check that my wallet is closed.
6. Might use a dirty towel (again—feared insomnia)- Use a clean towel after brushing my teeth.
7. Use clean towel after washing my face. (to prevent insomnia)
8. Someone might break in and kill me and my family- Make sure all downstairs doors are locked.
9. I might have left an appliance on and cause the deaths of my entire family- Make sure stove, microwave, oven, and toaster are off.
10. Someone might break in and kill me and my family- Make sure the front door of house is locked.
11. Someone might break in and kill me and my family- Make sure the alarm is on.

12. Someone might break in and kill me and my family- Check under my bed before going to bed.
13. God might be mad at me- Say my prayers correctly.

The scariest thing for me was saying my prayers wrong. I didn't want to upset God, and just having the *thought* I might upset God made me fear I would not sleep. As I considered the daunting list, and imagined NOT acting on my compulsions, the sensation often felt like a gun to the head. Again, the above is just a brief cross-section of my rituals, but it illustrates the terrifying fear I was facing and the behaviors I was doing to reduce that gun-to-the-head sensation. At this stage of ERP therapy, attempting to sit and resist a compulsion was no different from Lewis Carroll's Alice standing up to the violent "off with his head!" Queen of Hearts.

Identifying Our Fears

When we do a compulsion, when we check, when we ritualize, we need to identify *why* we are driven to do these things. What would happen if we did not engage in these behaviors? What are the obsessions that lead us to perform the compulsions? What are the feared outcomes? Once we know the why (and there may be more than one), we are better able to resist our compulsions.

Even as that little girl who obsessively counted the dwindling hours until morning, my fear was I wouldn't sleep. It didn't help that my father regularly whined he was going to "die" if he didn't get some sleep; it didn't help that, throughout my childhood and into young adulthood, he would scrutinize my face in the morning and say, "You look like crap. You didn't sleep last night, did you?" It didn't help that my parents' mantra of "You can't make it without us" replayed like a broken record in my head. In my irrational mind, the end of my relationship with them put into question my ability to function—specifically, to sleep.

Not surprisingly, all of my rituals and compulsions, all of my pulls to check, check and check again stemmed from this irrational, obsessive thought I wouldn't sleep *unless* I did them. As you can see from my hierarchy, not doing some rituals was easier than not doing others. In other words, some rituals had become more "important" than others.

I strongly encourage you to take some time and write down all of the things you do to make your fears go away or to reduce your anxiety. Naming them makes them weaker. Naming them empowers you. Naming them will ultimately give you control over them. Make a list of all of your rituals and observe the changes in your mind and body as you do. By taking action, by bringing the shadows of OCD into the light, you are mastering; you are climbing out of the rabbit hole!

List of my rituals:

_____

_____

_____

_____

_____

_____

We gain strength, and courage, and confidence by each experience
in which we really stop to look fear in the face…we must
do that which we think we cannot.

—Eleanor Roosevelt

The "What If?" Game

Morgan considered my list soberly before asking me a question that left me desperate to flee her office. "So what would happen if you didn't sleep?"

"I wouldn't function. I'd probably get sick, and then I wouldn't be able to take care of my family. Over time, I'd lose friends because I'd probably be acting crazy from sleep deprivation."

"And then what?" Morgan asked with a cryptic smile on her calm face.

"My husband would eventually leave me because I could no longer function and was certifiably nuts."

"And then what?"

"Well, I'd probably be committed. Maybe my now ex would come and visit me with our children. But eventually, I would die from lack of sleep. My epitaph would read: *Loving Wife and Mother Who Finally Got the Rest She Needed.*

By the time I was telling Morgan I'd be committed, I was no longer anxious to leave her office. Instead, I was laughing. Hearing my biggest fear voiced and theoretically played out made it seem silly and downright comical.

Talking or writing about your biggest fear(s) is wonderful ammunition against OCD. Morgan pointed out that while it was unlikely I would die from sleep deprivation, it was important to *sit* with the possibility and *not do* anything about this fear.

My next assignment: make a list of **alternative thoughts and beliefs** regarding my big fear. Here was my list:

1. Sleep is a natural function of the human body.
2. If I fight sleep, my body will eventually take over.
3. I am actually a wonderful sleeper.
4. If I don't sleep well tonight, I'll catch up by taking a nap or going to bed earlier tomorrow night.
5. I have never *not* functioned from a bad night of sleep.
6. Doctors often need to work in thirty-six hour shifts, performing major surgeries, before getting any sleep.

I encourage you to give this a try. Make a list of alternative thoughts and beliefs for your biggest fear(s). You will be amazed at how quickly the anxiety subsides and, simultaneously, how empowered you will feel! By facing our fear(s), they grow smaller; by taking action (e.g. writing this list) the OCD "pulls" will begin to fade.

My biggest fear is: _____

Alternate thought 1. _____

Alternate thought 2. _____

Alternate thought 3. _____

Alternate thought 4. _____

Alternate thought 5. _____

My life has been filled with terrible misfortune;
most of which never happened.
—Michel de Montaigne

Sheri does a great job describing the early stages of Exposure and Response Prevention (ERP) treatment for OCD. First, it is important to make an exhaustive list of all obsessions (fears) and compulsions (rituals) and avoidances (things a person avoids which might cause OCD anxiety) that exist in your life. As Sheri explains, her two main fears or "core" fears were:

1) She would not be able to sleep at night.
2) Her first husband was going to return from the dead and punish her.

We can see how these fears developed over her lifetime and the behaviors that became associated with making her feel "okay" about being able to sleep and feel safe in her home. Over time, she feared that if she did not perform these rituals, she would never sleep or Jon would "come and get" her and eventually, she would die. It is important to note that although doing the rituals reduced her fear *for that moment*, the fear *always returned*. Remember: compulsive behavior only *temporarily* reduces anxiety; it is only a poorly-functioning Band-Aid™.

The types of fears people with OCD experience are wide-ranging and varied. As discussed earlier, there tend to be eight different OCD "themes" fears can be lumped into. Within each of these, however, the kinds of fears are endless. For example, Sheri's OCD would be categorized in the "fear of harm to self" category. Below is a brief (and by no means exhaustive) questionnaire regarding some of the fears within each obsessional theme.

Identifying Your Obsessional Theme(s)

Read through the following questions and check the ones you recognize within yourself.

* Contamination:
- o Am I excessively concerned or worried about dirt, germs, or certain illnesses?
- o Am I excessively concerned or do I feel disgust about any bodily waste or secretions?
- o Am I excessively concerned I am going to be poisoned by household cleaners?
- o Do I worry excessively about any environmental hazards such as radiation or asbestos?
- o Do I have excessive fears the bodily waste or disease of animals or insects will cause harm to me or someone else?
- o Am I excessively bothered by sticky things I come into contact with?
- o Am I excessively worried about any dirt, germs, or contaminants just because they make me feel dirty or bad?

Harm to Self (Fear of harm that will come to yourself):
- o Am I excessively afraid harm will come to me and I will somehow be responsible?
- o Do I oftentimes fear I might lose control and harm myself?
- o Do I oftentimes have images come into my mind about violent or horrible things happening to me?
- o Am I oftentimes afraid I will do something embarrassing or out of control?
- o Am I oftentimes afraid I will forget to do something and it will cause harm to me?

Harm to Others (Fear of harm that will come to someone else):
- o Am I excessively afraid I may lose control and harm someone?
- o Am I excessively afraid I will accidentally forget to do something (e.g., turn off the stove) and something bad will happen to someone else?

- o Am I excessively worried I will hurt others by using insults or obscenities?
- o Do I oftentimes worry I will steal something?
- o Am I excessively afraid I will be responsible for something bad happening to others?

Sexual thoughts (Sexual concerns):
- o Do I have frequent, unwanted sexual thoughts, images, or impulses?
- o Am I excessively afraid I will act out sexually against others?
- o Am I excessively worried I will unintentionally cause sexual harm to someone by not being careful enough?
- o Am I excessively worried I may either be homosexual or act on homosexual impulses?

Magical/superstitious:
- o Do I worry excessively about breaking a superstitious belief that will then cause something bad to happen?
- o Do I have excessive concerns about certain numbers (lucky/unlucky) or words?

Somatic (health):
- o Do I worry excessively about becoming ill or contracting a disease?
- o Do I excessively worry I might be ill and not yet know it?

Scrupulosity (Concerns with right/wrong/morality):
- o Am I worried excessively about my thoughts and/or behaviors being wrong or amoral?
- o Am I worried excessively about blasphemy or somehow offending God?
- o Am I worried excessively I am a bad person or morally corrupt?
- o Am I worried excessively I am an evil person and possibly aligned with an evil entity (Devil, Satan).

Not Just Right:

- Am I excessively concerned about symmetry, order or how things are arranged?
- Do I oftentimes feel things have to be even, uneven, or matched?
- Do I worry excessively I might have lost something or I will lose something?
- Do I worry excessively about past events?
- Do I have an excessive need to know or remember things?
- Do I feel things have to be "just right" or I have to feel "just right" before moving on?
- Do I have an excessive fear of saying or thinking certain things?
- Do I have an excessive fear of not saying just the right thing?
- Do I have excessive thoughts I can prevent something bad from happening by performing some action?
- Do I oftentimes feel I need to count things?
- Do I oftentimes feel I need to visually scan my environment in a certain way?

* Questions listed are not published, but were developed for the self-help website (www.OCDChallenge.com) available through The Peace of Mind Foundation (www.PeaceofMind.org).

What theme(s) does your OCD fall into? Write these themes down in the space below. Some people only have one OCD theme, while others have many. Writing down your OCD Themes will help you to distill mentally the fears driving your behavior. Identifying your fears launches your road map to recovery.

My OCD Themes:

1.

2.

3.

4.

5.

Sheri's OCD Themes:
1. Fear of harm to self
2. Scrupulosity
3. Contamination

One sees great things from the valley,
only small things from the peak.

—G.K. Chesterton

Assessment of Insight

A key component in the initial evaluation of a person with OCD is the assessment of insight. Insight refers to how able a person is to see her OCD behavior as illogical. For example, on one level, Sheri believed her checking rituals were assisting her with sleep and safety, but when questioned about what would *really* happen if she did not engage in these rituals, she was able to see her beliefs were absurd. However, not everyone with OCD has this level of insight. Some people believe, for example, their hand washing rituals actually keep them from catching all kinds of diseases. They believe their washing is a good thing, regardless of the consequences to their bodies, (e.g. sore, chapped hands). Individuals present for treatment with a wide range of insight: some people know their rituals are absurd, but they feel compelled to do them, while others believe terrible things would happen if they did not engage in these repetitive behaviors. **Regardless of one's level of insight, treatment can be successful for all people with OCD.** However, when working with people who have low levels of insight, it is sometimes more difficult to get them to engage in the response prevention portion (not doing rituals) of the treatment because their fears have become so strong, based upon these faulty beliefs.

Ask yourself:

- What is your level of insight?
- How much do you actually believe your rituals are helping you?
- If you did not do your rituals, how much do you believe the feared consequences (obsessions) would happen?

Sometimes it is helpful to give yourself a belief rating. What percent of you believes your ritual will actually prevent the bad outcome from happening? For example, you may believe fifty percent that not washing your hands can give you AIDS, yet you still engage in repetitive hand washing. In this case, your belief score would be a fifty. What is your belief score? Are you performing rituals based upon assumptions you don't even believe? If you are, you are not alone.

What Are You Really Afraid Of?

It is important to look at the notion of fear a bit more closely. Sometimes it is actually the experience of fear itself (racing heart, perspiration, tense muscles, etc.) that a person is uncomfortable with, rather than the reported "feared outcome." In fact, when she actually is exposed to the feared outcome, negligible fear is reported. In Sheri's case, her feared outcome is not being able to sleep. In reality however, if she were prevented from sleeping she would probably have mild anxiety. What really gets her going though is the fear or discomfort associated with the fear she will not be able to sleep. All of Sheri's rituals are performed to reduce her fear of not being able to sleep, not to improve her chances of sleep. This is a subtle difference I know, but for many people it is a profound one. Habituating to or "getting used to" the fear or discomfort associated with the fear is what is most helpful.

A journey of a thousand miles begins with a single step.

—Lao Tzu

Wisdom is knowing what to do next; virtue is doing it.

—David Star Jordan

What Do You Do When Fear Comes to Visit?

Just as there are a number of obsessional themes, there are a multitude of compulsions or rituals that tend to occur in response to these fears. Here is a list of questions that may help to identify relevant, compulsive behaviors. As you take this questionnaire, focus on the theme areas you wrote down on your previous page entitled "My OCD Themes."

* Contamination theme:
- o Do I frequently or excessively wash my hands?
- o Do I shower more than most people or in a specific way, order, or duration?
- o Do I excessively brush or care for my teeth?
- o Do I excessively wash objects such as keys, wallet, or cell phone?
- o Do I frequently have my house checked for environmental hazards?
- o Do I avoid touching certain things?
- o Do I avoid going to certain places?
- o Do I avoid being around certain people for fear of becoming contaminated?
- o Do I use hand sanitizer frequently or excessively?
- o Do I follow a certain routine while washing hands or showering?

- Do I touch certain things only with the use of towels or gloves?

Harm to self theme:
- Do I frequently or excessively check any type of locks, windows, or doors to make sure they are closed or locked?
- Do I frequently or excessively check emails I am going to send or have sent?
- Do I frequently or excessively check household appliances to make sure they are turned off, e.g., stove, oven, iron?
- Do I check to make sure I have not made a mistake?
- Do I check to make sure I have not stolen something?
- Do I think, say, or imagine certain things to reduce violent images or thoughts?
- Do I avoid certain situations in which I am concerned I will lose control and hurt myself, e.g., high places, streets?
- Do I avoid people, places or situations for fear of embarrassing myself?
- Do I repeatedly ask or check for reassurance that something bad did not happen?
- Do I need to follow a certain routine because it will prevent harm or disasters from occurring?

Harm to others theme:
- Do I frequently or excessively check any type of locks, windows, or doors to make sure they are closed or locked?
- Do I frequently or excessively check emails that I am going to send or have sent?
- Do I frequently or excessively check household appliances to make sure they are turned off, e.g., stove, oven, iron?
- Do I frequently or excessively check to make sure I have not made a mistake?
- Do I frequently or excessively check to make sure I have not stolen something?

- o Do I think, say, or imagine certain things to reduce violent images or thoughts?
- o Do I avoid certain situations in which I am concerned I will lose control and hurt someone else, e.g., using knives, guns, or being around water?
- o Do I avoid people, places or situations for fear of embarrassing myself?
- o Do I repeatedly ask or check for reassurance something bad did not happen?
- o Do I need to follow a certain routine because it will prevent harm or disasters from occurring?
- o Do I frequently or excessively check to make sure I did not hit someone or something while driving?

Sexual thoughts theme:
- o Do I engage in mental rituals to reduce forbidden sexual thoughts?
- o Do I avoid certain people, places, or objects for fear of acting out sexually?
- o Do I engage in washing behaviors to reduce sexual concerns?
- o Do I avoid or feel uncomfortable interacting with people of the same sex for fear of acting out homosexual impulses?
- o Do I avoid or feel uncomfortable being around children for fear of saying or doing something sexually inappropriate?
- o Do I worry I might have done something sexually inappropriate and check or perform some action to reduce these concerns?
- o Do I frequently or excessively check to make sure I did not act out sexually or do something that would inadvertently (or advertently) have a sexual impact on another person?

Superstitions theme:
- o Do I avoid unlucky numbers or numbers that make me feel uncomfortable?
- o Do I like certain numbers or multiples of those numbers?
- o Do I have a preference for even or odd numbers?
- o Do I like or dislike certain colors or shapes?
- o Do I avoid challenging superstitious beliefs, such as walking under ladders or breaking mirrors?
- o Do I engage in any type of "game" such as not stepping on cracks?
- o Do I engage in a routine "game" to prevent something bad from happening?
- o Do I engage in certain behaviors that I feel will prevent bringing me bad luck?
- o Do I engage in mental rituals that I believe will keep "good luck" with me or will keep "bad luck" away?
- o Do I engage in mental rituals I believe will prevent bad things from happening to me or people I love?

Somatic theme:
- o Do I frequently go to the doctor to get things checked out?
- o Do I consult the internet, medical books, etc. to get information about illnesses/diseases I am concerned about?
- o Do I frequently or excessively check my body parts for changes or abnormalities?
- o Do I take frequent or unnecessary precautions to prevent/avoid illnesses or diseases?

Morality/Scrupulosity theme:
- o Do I read religious books (Bible, Torah, Koran) to please God?
- o Do I pray excessively?
- o Do I avoid places, objects, or situations that pertain to the Devil, Satan or things against my religion?

- Do I avoid saying things because they may be a lie?
- Do I engage in activities to show myself or others I am a moral person?
- Do I confess bad things I have done or may have done to feel better?

Not just right theme:
- Do I tap, touch, or rub things to even up or to feel better?
- Do I repeat actions, e.g., flipping the light switch on and off, until I feel just right?
- Do I look up information because of a need to know?
- Do I write things down or repeat them because of a need to remember?
- Do I avoid saying things for fear of not saying the "right" thing?
- Do I have to have things a certain way to feel just right?
- Do I avoid doing things because I know it may make me feel uncomfortable?
- Do I count things?
- Do I have to put things in a certain order or arrange them in a particular way to feel okay about them?
- Do I re-read words, sentences, paragraphs?
- Do I engage in frequent erasing or re-writing of things that don't look or feel right?
- Do I engage in excessive list making?

* Questionnaire was not published, but was developed for the self-help website www.OCDChallenge.com available through The Peace of Mind Foundation (www.PeaceofMind.org).

A note on ritualistic behaviors: not all rituals are a problem. Most everyone has some rituals, e.g., praying, using a "lucky toothbrush," bouncing the tennis ball three times before serving it, etc. Just because a behavior is ritualistic does not mean that it is OCD. Rituals can be comforting habits or idiosyncratic behaviors that exist without any impact on a person's life. OCD involves compulsive behaviors that MUST be performed to reduce anxiety. The general rule is if a person engages in a ritualistic behavior less than an hour a day and this behavior does not interfere with her ability to function in life, then it is likely not a problem.

In order to address OCD rituals, those that happen more frequently and intensely **and** cause significant problems, you will first need to fully understand all of the behaviors you engage in to satisfy your fears. Remember, these behaviors may seem like they are helping, but like a Band-Aid™, the assistance is temporary and superficial. Go through each theme area, and make a list of all of the rituals you do in each area. The list provided is certainly NOT exhaustive, so add in any behaviors which are not there. It would be very unlikely that all of your OCD behaviors would be listed. You may want to keep working on this list for a period of time, maybe a week or so, to identify behaviors that occur over time. Sometimes we forget about things until they happen, and only then are we reminded of them. When doing treatment, a complete list of all OCD behaviors is important so no compulsion goes unaddressed.

List of OCD Rituals (by theme):

1. Obsessional Theme:
   a. Ritual
   b. Ritual
   c. Ritual
   d. Ritual
   e. Ritual

2. Obsessional Theme:
    a. Ritual
    b. Ritual
    c. Ritual
    d. Ritual
    e. Ritual

The best way out is always through.

—Robert Frost

What we know about treatment for OCD is, for the most part, cognitive therapy alone is not sufficient. Just telling a person who has contamination fears that it is okay to touch the doorknob usually has very little benefit. It is likely this person will either doubt you are right or will doubt you know what you are talking about. She may even doubt she has OCD! It is very difficult to convince a person with OCD that something is okay to do, especially if it means breaking a ritual. A better option is to encourage her to "test" her beliefs. If I ask this person to touch the doorknob, without washing her hands afterward, for ten times a day and then see what happens, we will begin to see change take place. Not only will she get used to feeling the anxiety or discomfort resulting from touching the feared doorknob (habituation), but she will *learn* it really is okay (cognitive change). The process of *not* getting sick, or whatever it is she fears, eventually causes the belief to change. Now we're cooking!

Exposure (touching the feared doorknob) and Response Prevention (not washing hands afterward) is the only way to change beliefs or fears. Knowing this, how do we proceed? The next step in ERP is to have the client make an exposure hierarchy. Much like Sheri's hierarchy of fears and rituals, we would make a hierarchy of exposure tasks: "Do's" to help change behaviors and, eventually, beliefs. Then, we would make a list of response prevention tasks or "Don'ts" to represent the rituals or compulsions that are no longer allowed. Sheri's "Do" list might look something like this:

1. Leave a light on downstairs.
2. Leave front door to bedroom unlocked.
3. Lay purse on its side.
4. Leave purse open.
5. Leave wallet open.
6. Use a used/"dirty" towel for brushing teeth.
7. Use a used/"dirty" towel for washing face.
8. Let my husband lock downstairs doors.
9. Do not check to make sure the stove, microwave, oven and toaster are off.
10. Let my husband lock the front door.
11. Leave the alarm off.
12. Do not check under bed before going to bed.
13. Say prayers incorrectly.

Her "don't" list might look like this:

1. Don't check lights.
2. Don't check door locks.
3. Don't move purse.
4. Don't go back and close purse.
5. Don't close wallet.
6. Don't re-brush teeth after using a dirty towel.
7. Don't re-wash face after using the dirty towel.
8. Don't check to make sure the stove, microwave, oven and toaster are off.
9. Don't turn on the alarm.

10. Don't check under bed before going to bed.
11. Don't re-say prayers.

Right now your anxiety might be rising even thinking about doing or not doing these things. In therapy, however, we start easy, and then move up to harder tasks. I always want my clients to experience success and to begin building confidence from the start of treatment. A mistake I frequently hear other therapists make (usually from my clients who have experienced treatment failure) is asking clients to perform tasks that are too hard at the start of treatment. As a result, the client feels frustration, overwhelming anxiety and, ultimately, feelings of failure. It is better to start with the easiest possible task to ensure feelings of success early on, thereby engaging the client in treatment.

Sheri might start with leaving a light on downstairs every night for a week. I would have her rate how high her anxiety is each night on a scale of 1-10 (with 1 being very low anxiety and 10 being extreme anxiety). I would want to see if, over time, her anxiety becomes less and less with repetition. As stated earlier, we call this lessening of anxiety over time "habituation." After repeated exposure, your body "habituates" or "gets used to" the fear and will react with lower and lower levels of anxiety. Some people experience this process quickly, and others need more time to experience habituation. It is important to note **a critical ingredient for successful habituation is repetition**. The more you practice, the easier it gets and the faster this process will progress.

Now, it is important to note that Sheri's primary fear is the fear of not getting sleep. Many of you are saying, "The real exposure would be to have her stay up all night and see what happens." This is exactly correct. The real exposure for Sheri to face is not sleeping for one or more nights and seeing what happens. All of these rituals are, seemingly, to prevent insomnia. What if we ensured insomnia? Would all of the feared outcomes happen?

CHAPTER 6
Ripping off the Band-Aid

Refuse to act on an obsession, and it will die of inaction.
—Recovery Inc.

"'Hold your tongue!' said the Queen, turning purple.
'I won't!' said Alice.
'Off with her head!' the Queen shouted at the top of her voice.
Nobody moved.
'Who cares for you?' said Alice, (she had grown to her full size
by this time.) 'You're nothing but a pack of cards!'"

*— **Alice's Adventures in Wonderland**,* **Lewis Carroll**

When our son was little older than a toddler, he would receive the usual scratches and scrapes that come with the territory of early childhood. Regardless of how minor the boo-boo, he always asked for a Band-Aid™. Somehow, seeing the Spiderman covering on his skin made him feel better. In the beginning I would humor him, plastering knees and elbows that were merely bruised. But as he inched closer to kindergarten, I decided it was time to tell him the truth: Band-Aids™ are only necessary for open cuts and wounds. He didn't like this answer. He wanted his Spiderman Band-Aids™. He had grown accustomed to those Marvel Comic® plasters. You might even argue that he had become dependent upon the false psychological comfort of those cartoon coverings.

It wasn't until I explained to our son how our skin needs oxygen to breathe that he stopped asking for his favorite Band-Aid™. It was this realization, this *insight* that the Band-Aid™ could actually prevent healing, which helped him give it up.

OCD is like that special Band-Aid™. It woos you into thinking if you just stick with it, you will be safe, protected and healthy. But just like that Band-Aid™, it is actually preventing you from living your fullest life. And the longer you hold onto that Band-Aid™, the harder it will be to take it off and finally breathe on your own.

Morgan says that some patients find ripping off the Band-Aid™ of OCD works best; others prefer the slow and steady route. There is no right or wrong way to resist the pull of rituals or compulsions. **The key is to resist the very things the bully tells you to do.**

At this point in my therapy work, I am a cold turkey, rip-off-that-Band-Aid™ person. But years ago, when I started out with Morgan, I was a cautious, dip-one-toe-into-the-water-first kind of patient. Experiment and see what works best for you.

With my hierarchy of rituals and exposures before me, Morgan suggested I go home and sit with not checking those downstairs lights. I take most of her suggestions as assignments, because the key to mastering OCD is to challenge it regularly. I can't emphasize this enough: **cognitive behavior therapy only works if you put the time and effort into it.**

The following gives you an idea of my early experience with exposure work:

It's 10 PM and the lights are out in the bedroom. I am in bed! I did it! I didn't check those lights downstairs! I am so proud of myself! But now wait…did I make sure my flat iron was off? The instructional video for the flat iron said it was very important to make sure the flat iron is left unplugged…crap! There's the familiar rush of adrenaline…I feel this enormous pull to get up and check that flat iron…let me just do that and then I promise not to check the lights are on downstairs…

I sit up in bed, suddenly aware of a humming in the room. Great—now the computer is probably still on…okay, I'll just turn that computer off and then turn off the flat iron—then I'll hop back in bed.

I turn the computer off and feel a palpable release. Then it's on to the bathroom. Whew! The flat iron was already unplugged—release. It's time to get back to bed. I lie down, my veins filling with a mixture of relief and adrenaline. I am no longer thinking about the flat iron, computer or downstairs' lights and feel very proud of myself again—until I realize my wallet may still be open. I try to sit with this, but eventually I give in. I return to bed. My last thought before sleep takes over is wondering if I left the purse on its side.

No Exchanges or Refunds

When I shared my early experiences with exposure to Morgan, I felt confused. Part of me felt proud (*Yeah! I didn't check those downstairs lights!*), and the other part of me felt like a big failure (*I checked and checked and checked until I was exhausted—what have I accomplished?*).

Morgan was proud of me. I had tried to sit with my first exposure and that was something.

"Tried?? But I *did* sit with it! I never checked those lights. I never even thought about them!"

"Actually, you didn't sit with your anxiety, you fixed it by just swapping it for something else," Morgan said.

"But it felt like I was going to die if I didn't check that flat iron!"

"Killing OCD often feels like you are dying," she added, a sober smile on her face.

The voice of OCD actually gets louder and more demanding when you are ignoring it. As OCD is the "Doubting Disease," it thrives on your uncertainty and discomfort and wants nothing more than for you to fail. When you give into your rituals, OCD gets bigger and stronger.

The key to successful exposure is sitting with the pain and discomfort and knowing it will eventually pass.

Morgan says that the average time for someone to go through an *initial* exposure is approximately forty minutes. This means that it takes about forty minutes for the anxiety (that comes with doing an exposure) to abate. It looks like a bell curve where the anxiety peaks at a mid-point and shortly thereafter, subsides. The more often we engage in exposure activities, the faster we "habituate" to the anxiety and, thus, the shorter in duration and intensity our bell curve gets.

OCD is stealthy. Just when you are focused and determined to give up one ritual or compulsion, it throws another one at you and makes you feel like its command is a matter of life and death. Do not give in to this persistent bully! Do not negotiate with this "terrorist!" He will only try to bargain with you for more rituals or compulsions. Let him rant and rave all he wants to about exchanging this ritual for that compulsion—his desperation is a sure sign he is growing weaker.

Don't Get Comfortable

In order to keep OCD at bay, I regularly need to challenge myself with exposures. Living a life free of OCD means living a life where we are **comfortable with being uncomfortable**. That misfiring in my brain continues to come up with new things for me to ritualize and check, but just as Morgan predicted in the beginning of my treatment, the bully's voice has grown fainter and is no longer something I take seriously. The longer I continue to sit with exposures, the greater freedom I experience; the longer I resist putting on that unnecessary Band-Aid™, the more OCD's pulls become nothing more than weak (albeit annoying) taps on my psychological back.

Watching OCD Die: What Regular Exposure Brings

Since I went the entire night without checking the downstairs lights, I felt empowered to move onto my second exposure: resisting the urge to check that the bedroom door was locked. Morgan immediately suggested I go home that night and purposely leave the door unlocked. GULP!

"I can't do that," I said, my heart already racing at the mere *thought* of leaving the door unlocked.

She insisted I could, but these were early days and I still preferred putting that one toe in the water instead of my entire body. Because I was still at the "embryo" stage of exposure treatment, I decided to lock the door and only check it once. I considered it a mini-step in the right direction.

Armed with the knowledge that sitting with my anxiety and discomfort were key, armed with the previous experience of exposure, I felt confident, ready to "take on" my OCD. Here's what that second exposure felt like:

The bedroom door is locked and I am in bed with the lights off. Already, I am doubtful I really locked it and it occurs to me Morgan is right, I never should have locked it in the first place—assuming I even did. I try to remember the faint click of the lock as I pressed my thumb against its raised button. Yes, yes I am almost certain that I heard it click. But what if by some small chance I didn't lock it?

I take a deep breath and decide to get out of bed and grab a piece of paper and pen. I scribble a quick account of a worst case scenario as I had verbally done with Morgan:

I leave the door unlocked. A burglar might enter our home and now we are unprotected. Well, no. If a burglar entered our home the dog would start barking like crazy and our alarm system would go off.

I put down the paper and realize I am even more worked up now than I was just sitting in the dark! What if that alarm isn't on?

I want nothing more than to check that the alarm is on—then I can relax and just drift off to sleep. Suddenly, it occurs to me I am no longer thinking about our bedroom door being locked. The bully is trying to distract me and keep me focused on other things. BUT I AM NOT GOING TO LISTEN TO THAT TERRORIST THIS TIME!

I lie back down in bed. I want nothing more than to ask my husband for reassurance. It would be so easy to poke him a couple of times and ask him to confirm the alarm is most definitely, positively, without a doubt ON; it is so painfully tempting to get out of bed and push that lock down until my thumb bruises. My heart is racing; I have enough adrenaline to lift a car; I feel like I'm dying. But I refuse to do what OCD tells me to do and that's when something amazing happens!

My OCD is shouting at me now, telling me that I'd better check under the bed; there were workers in our home earlier today and what if one of them decided to wait under our bed and attack us while we are sleeping? Ah-ha! This is what Morgan was talking about! OCD is screaming louder because it is growing weaker and, therefore, becoming more desperate!

Still, I feel like I am dying. The anxiety becomes too much for me and suddenly I feel like I am no longer in my body, like I am watching the bully bark orders at my brain, but I am not there. I am merely a spectator. A feeling similar to an engine roaring takes over as OCD continues to command I check the bathroom faucet is off, the computer is turned off, our closet light is off. I am dizzy and can no longer keep track of the terrorist's demands; I am too far away from its ranting to care. And before I know it, I am sound asleep.

You are much more than your mind. You may think that your mind is running the show, but that is only because you have trained your mind to think this way....Your mind is a tool for you to use in any way you wish. The way you now use your mind is only a habit, and habits, any habits, can be changed.

—*You Can Heal Your Life,* **Louise Hay**

Be a Reporter

I couldn't wait to meet with Morgan and share my recent success at sitting through my OCD's demands!

"It felt like an out of body experience! I felt like I was *watching* instead of participating," I gushed.

"You were a reporter. You observed what was going on, but you didn't get personally involved," she beamed.

Call it an out of body experience, call it being a reporter—one of the best tools I used for challenging OCD, for kicking that demanding bully to the curb, was to separate myself from OCD's relentless commands by becoming an observer of the experience. I purposefully distance myself when the anxiety from sitting with the exposure *feels* like it is too great to bear. By removing myself and mentally "checking out," I am able to observe and not judge what I am feeling, regardless of the intensity. I believe each of us has a Higher Self. It's that little voice inside of us that knows better; it's a voice devoid of fear. When we become reporters, when we merely observe and don't DO anything, OCD might throw us some curveballs (Did you check the stove? Are you *sure* your hands are clean?), but all we have to do is make a mental note of them: *Ah, here goes my OCD again, telling me to make sure the garage doors are down. And now it's telling me the oven may still be on. Let's see what else it's going to come up with...*

Reporters are objective observers; reporters tell the facts; reporters don't interpret and take action. **It's this inaction that weakens the faulty circuitry of OCD.**

I don't think a reporter should give advice or make predictions.
—**Peter Jennings**

The Advantage of Being a Reporter

Sheri talks about how becoming an objective reporter of her experience helped her to disengage from her anxiety. This is a very effective strategy that works for some people with OCD. The more we develop the skill of observing our experience, *without judgment*, the more we are able to tolerate it. This mode of thought comes from Eastern philosophy and is the cornerstone of the Mindfulness Movement in psychology. Mindfulness means to be aware of what you are experiencing, without reacting to or judging it. It is neither good nor bad a person is feeling anxiety, it simply is: racing heart, stiff muscles, lightheadedness, sweaty palms, shallow breathing, etc. Start by writing down your physical and emotional experiences during an exposure. An example taken from a client named "Amy" looked like this:

I have decided to walk out of the house and not check to see if I have locked the door. As soon as I begin to walk away from the door my heart is pounding, I experience feelings of fear that I have left my house vulnerable to a burglary. I now begin to think about all of the bad things that might happen if someone were to break-in. What is my body experiencing? I feel tightness in my chest, my heart is beating rapidly, I am compelled to return to check the door. I keep walking. Now I feel my ears ringing. Funny, that has never happened before...this is new. All of these feelings are normal and expected; my OCD is trying to convince me to return, but I will not listen. A thought pops in: "It might get worse;" I feel increased anxiety as I drive away. My body is shaking as I back out of the driveway. I drive away and do not return.

Notice how in this scenario the writer did not ever judge what she was experiencing. She never said, "This is really bad" or "This is going to kill me," but just described her experience. Try to report your experience. Do not start by "observing" an OCD exposure; this will be too hard. Instead, start with just observing a normal event, like doing the dishes. Maybe sit down and write about the events of doing the dishes, what the dishes look like, how the bubbles slide down the fork, how your feet feel after standing all day, etc. Just write about whatever you notice; this will help you understand what it is like to observe and report on an event. Research shows Mindfulness training helps a person to become an observer of her experience, and helps to protect her against negative feelings like anxiety and self-judgment. When you have become pretty good at it (without writing about your judgments about the event, e.g., I hate doing dishes), you will be ready to report on an exposure.

I have nothing to do with the selection of stories. I'm the reporter.
—Kate Adie

Take a moment to look over your OCD hierarchy. Imagine you are a reporter and choose one item on your list (e.g. touch the bottom of my shoe and not wash my hands) to sit with. As you sit, notice the physical, emotional and mental manifestations. Keep a journal handy to report exactly what is happening, without your ego's interpretation. You may find it easier to use a recorder. I have used a mini recorder in the past and found it to be very empowering to play back my observations.

Remember: OCD is irrational and therefore loves to feed off our warped interpretations or unfounded fears. **By remaining a reporter during an exposure, we grow stronger.** It is this renewed strength that allows us to sit for longer periods of time without performing our rituals and compulsions.

I can act my way into feeling better sooner than I can feel my way into acting better.

—O.W. Mower

Sheri is right in her approach to treatment for OCD: fears must be faced and rituals must be deliberately and intentionally avoided. For many people, this is quite difficult. Even the *thought* of facing a fear, allowing it to be there, and not performing the ritual to reduce the subsequent anxiety may seem impossible. When working with people in therapy, I spend a lot of time building rapport with a client and ultimately, establishing trust. My client must trust I will keep her safe, and I will not ask her to do something dangerous or inadvisable. The component of trust is vitally important because OCD treatment involves asking a person to do the opposite of what she believes is the right thing to do. My client must trust that:

a. I know what I am doing,

b. I understand the proper treatment approach for OCD, and

c. I would not ask a client to do anything that would put her in danger or at risk for danger.

Clearly, Sheri trusted her psychologist, Morgan, and was willing to initially try some things low on her hierarchy.

Gotta Go Through it!

There is a story I remember from childhood about "Going on a bear hunt," where you "can't go over it, can't go under it, can't go around it, gotta go through it." I believe this concept applies perfectly to the process of facing OCD. People commonly ask me, "Is this the only way? Isn't there another way to make my OCD go away?" The answer is that "you gotta go through it": **the only way to combat your OCD is to face it**, to go through the anxiety of *not* doing rituals and *not* giving into your fears; to learn the anxiety caused by not doing rituals *will not* kill you. Sheri described feeling like she was dying when she felt her OCD anxiety. This is not uncommon. It feels terrible to sit with your anxiety, but it *does get easier*! Each time you face your fears and don't do a ritual, it gets easier and you get stronger. As Sheri eloquently pointed out: it is your OCD dying, not you!

Building Your OCD Muscles

Have you ever done an exercise using muscles that you had not used in a while? Did your muscles get sore? This is a normal part of getting in shape, right? The same is true for fighting OCD. In the beginning, it is terrifying; it feels uncomfortable; it hurts to feel your anxiety; you want to run away. However, over time you will be able to do the exposure tasks without ritualizing and without feeling this uncomfortable pain. Eventually, you will not get "sore." Just as with continual exercise, where you get stronger and more able to perform harder and harder physical tasks, so it is with fighting your OCD. With regular exposure, you will be able to do more and more challenging things without feeling the "pain" you feel initially.

If you think about the development of your OCD as simply making connections in your brain, you can imagine over time that these connections become very well defined. For example, if you make the connection between feeling anxious and checking the door locks, then after years of checking, this connection will become very strong. You have literally burned a pathway in your brain so it feels automatic for the behavior of checking to follow the feeling of anxiety. To change this behavior, it will require forming new pathways in your brain, like building new bicep muscles. At first this will feel uncomfortable, because the new behavior (not checking) will require a different pathway. After continued repetition of anxiety followed by not checking, a new pathway begins to develop. This is important to understand because it highlights the importance of repetition in this process. It takes hundreds of repetitions of the new behavior to create these new, healthier pathways. Is it worth it? YES! To live a life without fears and rituals, without OCD rules and consequences, a life of freedom...yes, it is worth it.

The "Whack a Mole" Phenomenon

Sheri described what I call the "Whack a Mole" phenomenon. There is a childhood game called *Whack a Mole* where the child hits a little mole that pops up and down; however, just as that mole is pushed down, another pops up. The game is such that the child must continuously hit the moles as they pop up. Truthfully, I am not even sure if the game ever ends, and this perhaps makes the metaphor even more fitting. Just as you may face one fear, another will instantaneously pop up. Sheri describes this perfectly when she does her exposures. She is resisting the downstairs' light-checking ritual when almost immediately, her OCD tells her the flat iron may still be on. This is *so common!* OCD wants to win; it wants to stay alive. But the only way OCD can stay alive is if you feed it with your anxiety and rituals. When you start resisting rituals, it *will* start screaming about other things, things you may not have even thought about before…it does not want to die.

So what is the answer?

The answer is to keep pushing down those moles, to even expect they will pop up. Know that just as soon as you stop checking the stove, your OCD may throw a new fear at you. In fact, expect it will. This new fear may be in the same "theme" as the old one, or it may be completely new, like no other fear you have ever experienced.

Case in point: I was working with a man who was a rancher from a rural part of our state. He had contamination fears that he had successfully faced and was making great progress. One day he sat down in my office, his face taut with fear.

"I think I might be gay," he said.

Sensing his fear might be the "mole" talking, I asked, "Are you attracted to men?"

"No way! Not even close! I love women."

"Well? Why do you think you might be gay?"

"I just had this thought, 'What if I am gay?' and now I think I might be because I had that thought."

This is OCD! This is **how it works**. Just when you are working on "killing" a part of OCD, it fires off another, even more frightening, possibility. So your job is to accept that this is just a part of the process. If I go on a diet and lose 25 pounds, should I expect I will never crave chocolate ice cream again? Of course not! I know that throughout my life I will have urges, and cravings I will have to manage and keep in check. It is the same with OCD. You will have pulls and fears present themselves over the years, and your job is to recognize them for what they are: OCD.

A Prison with an Open Door

As you may have noticed, I love metaphors and have presented numerous ones throughout this book. In therapy, different metaphors resonate with different people, so I keep offering them until that specific one creates an "Aha" moment for him or her. So here is another one to think about: OCD is like being in a self-created prison with an open door you *feel* unable to walk through. In your metaphorical prison you are trapped, paralyzed by your fears, chained to your rituals and avoidances. Despite these horrible conditions, you feel safety in the "known" of this prison, the sense of control over your anxiety these rituals give to you. You are terrified to leave because even though there is freedom outside the door, there is also the unknown... the possibility of risk and danger. For years, if not decades, you have lived in this self-imposed prison which feels safe despite its hellish nature.

I encourage you to take a risk, to approach that open door and eventually walk out. I encourage you to face the perceived risks and dangers because what you will get in return is ultimate freedom and the ability to live outside the confines of this small place...to experience the fullness of your life.

CHAPTER 7
How to Avoid Falling Down the Rabbit Hole

Well, after this I should think nothing of falling down stairs.
— *Alice's Adventures in Wonderland,* **Lewis Carroll**

The chains of habit are too weak to be felt until they are too strong to be broken.
—**Samuel Johnson**

Jeff Garlin is Larry David's co-star and executive producer of the hit HBO comedy series, *Curb Your Enthusiasm,* who penned a memoir about his lifelong struggle to lose weight (*My Footprint: Carrying the Weight of the World*). Recently, I randomly turned on the radio and heard the talented comedian discussing his ongoing success with weight loss. Now, I am a thin woman who is blessed with a fast metabolism. Other than enjoying his HBO series, I had no obvious reason to keep the Sirius station tuned into Mr. Garlin's advice for shedding and keeping off extra pounds. But I found myself drawn to his words of struggle and success—they were resoundingly similar to my struggles and success with OCD.

Jeff Garlin refers to himself as a food addict. To the comedian, there is no such thing as a "little piece of cake." According to 20/20, Garlin says, "There is no 'I'll have a little taste.' That does not exist. It's not possible....I know, one taste and I'm on my way to death."

Sound familiar?

OCD and food addiction are both emotional disorders manifesting in compulsive behavior. Listening to Jeff's struggle to control his irrational yearning to over-eat made me feel I wasn't alone in my inner-battle of willpower. And just like Jeff, I had the power to succeed.

Garlin now weighs between 260 and 270 pounds, down from his peak weight of 320; I do between 5-10 minutes of compulsions per day, down from a peak of almost two hours. Neither is curable, but both are highly treatable.

Like Jeff Garlin, it was important for me to learn the pitfalls and danger zones of OCD. Garlin knows to stay away from fast food and sugar—his two big weaknesses. Morgan helped me discover OCD's insidious traps to avoid for continued success. When we can recognize our personal Achilles' heel that triggers OCD, we are better able to prevent ourselves from falling down the rabbit hole of rituals and compulsions. Below are OCD's most common tricks.

Getting Comfortable

A good week ago, I was feeling quite proud of myself as my compulsions were down to a mere five minutes per day. Each time a pull to check something emerged, I sat with it and, eventually, my OCD quieted down. A good portion of the time, the pull to check something was barely more than a quiet nudge. I was in a great place. And so I thought I "deserved" a day off from fighting the pulls.

Big mistake! Remember: when we get comfortable, OCD finds an opportunity to get stronger. It's no different from Jeff Garlin having a little dessert. There's no such thing as a little taste or a harmless check for food addicts and individuals with OCD, respectively. We regularly need to starve OCD when it tells us what we "need" to do.

One important caveat worth noting is OCD's proclivity to all or nothing thinking. Sometimes we will give into a pull to ritualize or check. It's so important to recognize such slips for what they are: a mere weak moment, and nothing more. Slipping does not equal a guaranteed trip down the abysmal OCD rabbit hole; slipping is not synonymous with failing. Rather, like so much in life, it is our attitude toward our slip(s) that determines whether or not it remains just that or snowballs into a seemingly never-ending tango with OCD. **We always, always have the power to become that reporter and stop ourselves from making further slips.** The sooner we resist the next ritual or compulsion, the easier it will be to resist future pulls.

The night I weakened and checked to see if anything on the nightstand was going to fall off created that familiar "ah" sensation I had missed. Unfortunately, I immediately craved an even greater sense of (false) control. *Maybe I need to check the bureau, too? Now did I REALLY check to see the alarm clock isn't on the edge of the nightstand? And what about the fan light in our bathroom? What if that's on? I'll just check that quickly, too. Wait a second—is that faucet on? Let me just check and make sure...*

Thankfully, I was able to stop my rituals and compulsions within twenty minutes as I caught myself—mid-pull—and recognized where I'd gone wrong: the moment I got comfortable and thereby, gave myself permission to let my guard down. And just as Jeff Garlin explains that if he falls off the wagon of over-eating, it gets harder and harder to get back on, sitting with the pulls was that much more challenging after I fell off the wagon and checked that nightstand. **When it comes to OCD, DON'T GET COMFORTABLE!!!**

Complacency is a state of mind that exists only in retrospective: it has to be shattered before being ascertained.

—Vladimir Nabokov

Don't let your special character and values, the secret that you know and no one else does, the truth - don't let that get swallowed up by the great chewing complacency.

—Aesop

Sheri does a great job describing complacency or getting to a "comfortable place" with her OCD and how this is a common pitfall. Complacency appears in two common ways:

(1) The OCD is better when it comes to the low to moderately frightening exposure tasks, (e.g. the exposures that are from 1-7 on the hierarchy); but you are not wanting to face the exposures that are 8-10 on the hierarchy.
or
(2) The OCD is much better, e.g. she has reached the 9s and 10s on her hierarchy, but then she "relaxes" and allows herself to engage in the lower level rituals she had previously faced.

In the first form of complacency, OCD is better, but still there. Don't get me wrong, **we are not looking for perfection**. People who present for treatment are usually in acute distress, *and pain.* They are spending more than an hour a day with rituals and avoidances and are *miserable.* After working for a few weeks or months, things improve. Maybe they have more time in their life to do the things they enjoy or maybe they feel reduced anxiety and increased pleasure in life.

At this point, I see the desire to quit therapy emerge. Usually it is right before we get to the really hard stuff in the OCD hierarchy, the 9s and 10s. I completely understand: these things are hard to do and if you are feeling better, what the heck, maybe it is okay to just leave it where it is. Well, the problem with this decision to be "comfortable" or "complacent" with OCD too early is it leaves the door open for a re-emergence of obsessions and compulsions in the future.

I hate to say you can *never* get comfortable with your OCD, but it is very common for people to get comfortable too soon, *before they are ready.* As a treatment provider, I think of this as a medical model. Would a surgeon remove ninety percent of a tumor and leave the rest? Would he say, "I think I got enough; I hope the part I left in there doesn't start growing again." Of course not! And neither should you. When the desire to quit becomes evident, argue with it. When it tells you: "It's okay, you have done enough; why do the really hard ones?" you need to be prepared to say "I am *not* done. I have to finish this so it will not return. I will keep going." Although you may feel better when you achieve some success with your OCD, remember to keep going. Instead of stopping prematurely, before you do the hard exposures, see this as an opportunity to re-energize yourself to finish it off!

The second way complacency manifests itself is when a person gives herself permission to ritualize, often after making great strides in treatment. OCD may say to you: "You have been doing so well. What is one little ritual going to hurt? You deserve it!" As Sheri points out, this is a very dangerous conversation to have with yourself. A saying in Alcoholics Anonymous goes something like this: "One drink is too many and a thousand is never enough." OCD works somewhat like this. One *ritual* is too many and a thousand is never enough. While no one expects you to be perfect, and you will have goof ups along the way, fight the permission-giving thoughts by countering with statements like:

"I deserve to have a life!"

"I never do just one ritual."

"I need **not** to ritualize more than ever!"

When you change the way you look at things, the things you look at change.

—Dr. Wayne Dyer

Physical concepts are free creations of the human mind, and are not, however it may seem, uniquely determined by the external world.

—Albert Einstein

Cognitive Errors

The way we think about things creates our reality. Quantum physics is the study of life at the sub-atomic level. In the film, *What the Bleep Do We Know?*, physicists demonstrate that small particles of matter change based on whether or not there is an observer. We, the observer, literally affect and change the reality of the quantum world by interacting with it. So it makes sense that our thoughts, the way we perceive our reality, can actually CREATE our reality!

One popular quantum physics' experiment, the Double Slit, is one of the more well-known demonstrations of our effect on matter. When electrons, tiny particles of matter, are observed to go through two slits, the atoms create two succinct bands on the screen. However, when the electrons go *unobserved*, a pattern of interference occurs, creating wave-like patterns as they emerge through the slits. Bottom line: what we see literally affects our reality on the sub-atomic level.

Knowing our perception can influence our reality, it is important to be aware of our thoughts. The "Doubting Disease" that is OCD makes it easy to fall into false and negative ways of thinking; as a result, our reality is in danger of looking worse than it actually is. **It's important to remember you, the observer, always have the power to change your reality by changing your thoughts.**

Following is a list of several common cognitive errors. Some of these can be applied to other types of thoughts, not just obsessions, but this is how they applied to me:

Black and White Thinking

It was early morning. The sky was still dark, but I knew the time to rise was near. I turned over in bed and my hand brushed against something foreign and small: a bug! I studied it closely. Whatever it was, it was no longer among the living; whatever it was, I didn't want it in our bed! I put it on my nightstand and resisted the impulse to wash my hands. I remained in bed for the next forty-five minutes until the alarm went off, never making it back to blissful unconsciousness.

When I shared the bug exposure with Morgan, I couldn't help but notice the pride in her eyes. "You sat with the pull to wash your hands—wonderful!"

"But I failed. I never fell asleep again," I said.

"No, you didn't fail. Failing is getting up to wash your hands."

Ah. I'd just fallen prey to black and white, all or nothing false logic. Morgan went on to explain that there were other factors I wasn't taking into account:

I'd already slept for a good seven hours.

- I was relaxed as I lay in bed with the pull to wash my hands.
- One year prior, my heart raced at the mere thought of sitting with "dirty" hands.
- I could hear our children stirring in their beds.
- Suddenly, when Morgan pointed out all of these factors, my exposure didn't feel like a mark of failure, but rather a testament to my continued resistance to OCD's pulls.

It's important to note that the bug exposure took place a day before my session with Morgan. So my negative perception of the exposure, my black and white thinking, created a sense of failure that permeated my life for those twenty-four hours. And the "Doubting Disease" that is OCD thrives on weakness, so it is no surprise that my rituals and compulsions increased during this 24-hour window: my negative beliefs had changed my reality.

I recently met Suzanne for lunch and shared the bug exposure with her. I thanked her for writing about my awareness, my "insight" earlier on in this book, but I needed her to know that like many people who contend with OCD, I too lose my compass, my internal sense of what is and isn't rational.

"I'm curious, why did you feel the need to wash your hands after touching the bug?" she asked. "Are you afraid of bugs?" "Do you believe they're dirty?"

The truth is there is no rhyme or reason to why I felt compelled to wash my hands. No, I am not afraid of bugs. No, I don't think they're dirty. I just felt an irrational need to control.

Suzanne gave me a smile that made me think of teachers who catch their students cheating and said, "So you are not even sure why you wanted to wash your hands? Hmmm. I wonder what that was about?"

The sad answer is that logically, I have no idea. The *truth* is I was controlling my ANXIETY, not dirt or germs. So I may have insight on the emotional topography of my life, but when it comes to the reason behind my specific pulls and rituals, I have no logical answers to offer.

It doesn't matter why we feel compelled to do our rituals and compulsions; what matters is that we try not to do them. In other words, sometimes we have no logical clue why we are doing something or we think we have a clue, but the clue is ridiculous! The reality is what we are truly attempting to control is our anxiety. As we have learned, this control is fleeting and always leads to more and more anxiety. The only way to eradicate OCD is to allow anxiety to be present, to expect it will come, and to commit to NOT trying to make it go away. Simply stated, we have to try our best to resist our rituals. Making resistance a regular part of our lives is a healthy, reasonable goal—it doesn't mean we are expected to be perfect. Black and white thinking also creates a potential danger zone for low self-esteem. When we think in terms of all or nothing, we inadvertently set ourselves up for failure. Life is about trying our best and our best will change from day to day, moment to moment. It's when we are kind to ourselves, when we see our efforts as successes because we know we are doing our best that our perception morphs from an overwhelming tower of black and white to a warm landscape of vibrant colors.

Tell me to what you pay attention and I will tell you who you are.
—Jose Ortega y Gassett

Living With Uncertainty

Sheri talks about black and white thinking, with regard to being harsh and critical of herself, ultimately leading to reductions in self-esteem. But there is another angle to this all or nothing thinking pervasive in OCD: the need to know. People who suffer with OCD want to know *without a doubt*:

- my hands are either contaminated or not
- my stove is either on or off
- the door is either locked or unlocked
- I either killed a person while driving or I did not
- I either told a lie or I did not

Now, I understand in reality certain things are true absolutes, e.g. I did not leave the door "sort of" unlocked or the stove "kind of" on. **However, black and white thinking creeps in when we look for certainty**. I can be ninety-five percent sure I turned the stove off and feel fine with that. I can be reasonably sure I locked the front door when I left and not worry. People with OCD like to know *for sure* a thing is true. When one is not sure, up spikes the anxiety. The reason it is important to look at black and white thinking is **if you are only comfortable with the absolute, the one hundred percent certainty, you will always suffer**. Allowing the "gray area" to rest in your mind gets your brain, over time, comfortable with reasonable doubt. Tell yourself you can live with ninety percent certainty that you did not have a spelling error in your email; allow yourself to be comfortable with eighty-five percent confidence that your hands are clean; be okay with ninety-five percent assurance that the iron is unplugged. When you allow yourself to live in the gray area or as Sheri more accurately describes it, a "world of vibrant colors," life unfolds into a beautiful world of freedom.

Over-Felt Responsibility

A hallmark characteristic of people with OCD is "over felt" responsibility. This means people with OCD feel **more** responsible for the random events in life than people without OCD. Sound familiar? This means when "bad" things happen, people with OCD are at-risk for feeling like they are somehow responsible for the bad event. In addition, they may engage in behaviors to *actually prevent* future bad events from occurring. Although there is no connection between the behavior or ritual performed and the likelihood of the bad event happening, it just feels better to go ahead and perform the ritual, just in case.

One way out of this mind trap (that only leads to ever-more rituals) is to remind yourself that we, as humans, are primarily not at all in control of future misfortune. I can eat healthy, exercise, not smoke and wear sunscreen and *still get cancer*. Once I accept this is a possibility, I can start to heal. Performing hundreds of rituals each day to prevent cancer might make me feel better, but it has no impact whatsoever on whether or not I develop the disease (and it ruins my quality of life in the process).

Over-felt responsibility can be even more powerful when it involves the safety of another person, particularly a loved one. If a person believes not doing a ritual may result in harm to another person, she is stuck in an OCD trap. Again, she must accept she cannot possibly control random events through ritualistic

111

behavior. As Sheri and I have discussed in other chapters of this book, it is through testing these beliefs via behavioral change that our beliefs are ultimately changed.

Fortune Telling: OCD's Penchant for Portending Worst Case Scenarios

OCD loves to whisper awful predictions to me, particularly close to bedtime. Here are some of them:

If I don't check the front door is locked, I'll be up all night thinking about it and won't be alert for work the next day.

If I don't check the flat iron is tucked away safely, I will give an awful performance on stage.

If I don't go to check the stove is off, there will be a fire of catastrophic proportions.

Many times when the bully suggests these things, my insight is out of commission. So what can a person "sans rationality" do? Write down OCD's awful predictions and REPLACE them with a *What if?* that is positive. Again, our perception creates our reality so let's change our thoughts so we can enjoy a more pleasant reality!

Here's my replacement list:

If I don't check that front door, I can remain in my cozy bed. If I don't check that front door, I'm starving my OCD. By starving my OCD, I get stronger and gain my freedom back!

If I don't make sure the flat iron is tucked away, I maintain control, I remain in the driver's seat — not OCD. My performance has nothing to do with where that flat iron is and my performance will be better than ever because I sat with something uncomfortable.

If I don't check the stove is off, there may or may not be a fire. Fires are not in my control. Staying in bed IS in my control. By remaining in bed, my mind wanders from one concern to the next, begins to daydream and my anxiety decreases exponentially.

I strongly recommend you take a moment to list any awful predictions percolating in your head. You can do this now or when OCD gives you a jabbing tap on your back. Writing down our cognitive errors slows the anxiety surge because our thoughts multiply much faster inside our head than they do when we take the time to write them down. It's important you take the time to write down a positive, wonderful fortune/outcome for yourself. This will help you get off the negative train and create a new reality for yourself.

Fearing the Least Probable Outcome

Fortunetelling's first cousin is *fear of the least probable outcome*. With regard to OCD, this means being afraid of the thing least likely to happen, while ignoring the things that are obvious dangers. Remember the story my client told at the beginning of this book? He likened engaging with OCD as similar to betting all of his money on a bet he was sure to lose while ignoring the "sure" winner. This is exactly what fearing the least probable outcome embodies. For example, a client of mine had not visited the dentist in twenty-five years because of an irrational fear she would contract HIV from the dental equipment. I guess there is always going to be a remote, worst-case scenario in which her dentist neglected to clean his dental equipment after working on an active HIV patient, after which my client arrived at the dentist with an open sore in her mouth. The chances of all of these unlikely elements coming together were astronomical–less than a hundredth of a percent. However, the chances of this woman's teeth rotting were pretty high given her lack of dental hygiene and care for the past twenty-five years. Nevertheless, she put her "money" on the thing least likely to happen, not betting on the "obvious" winner.

Another patient of mine was a thrill seeker. He would parachute out of airplanes, travel to remote areas of Africa, invest millions of dollars in risky ventures, but he would not step on a crack in the pavement, step into a room with his left foot, or wear a certain tie on Tuesdays. Why? Because his superstitious OCD told him something bad *might* happen if he did these things. People with OCD often fear the thing least likely to happen and ignore the obvious, more probable dangers.

Take a look at your fears. When you examine them carefully, with a logical, reporter's mind, ask yourself:

- Are they likely to happen?
- What are the chances of these fears actually happening?
- Am I using logic when making my decisions regarding these fears?
- Are there things in my life that are greater potential dangers to me than the ones I spend my time fearing?

I bet there are.

Magical and Superstitious Thinking

Depend on the rabbit's foot if you will, but remember,
it didn't work for the rabbit.

—R.E. Shay

For years I believed if I didn't pray in a specific manner I'd be unsafe, vulnerable to bad things happening and potentially up all night. So I gave in—again and again. And the prayers and rules behind them grew stronger and stronger, until my prayer rituals were taking up to a half-hour at bedtime.

I have a friend who won't make love when a close family member is flying. She wasn't ever diagnosed with OCD, but this is definitely an example of magical or superstitious thinking. A man I know has a "lucky" deodorant he feels he must put on if he wants to ensure a successful day. Does he have OCD? I don't know and I don't think the answer matters. Many cultures in the world lend themselves to a bit of magical or superstitious thinking: knocking on wood, spitting to ward off the evil eye and putting an acorn near a window to keep lightning out, to name a few. Religions lend themselves to rituals: saying Hail Mary's, praying to Allah five times a day, welcoming the Sabbath with candles, wine, and challah. Let me be clear: I am NOT saying that simple rituals or religious customs are OCD or lead to OCD. These activities are part of our collective experience as humans and can be wonderful cultural events that give richness to our lives. What I am saying is that when we use magical thinking to reduce anxiety to the point WE MUST engage in rituals to reduce our spikes of anxiety, there could be a problem.

For me, doing the opposite of what my magical thoughts "said" to do kept me safe from relapse. When I felt the pull to say a specific prayer, I simply didn't say it. It was HARD—very, very HARD to do this. But I did it and I'm still alive! Fredrich

Nietzsche's famous quote: *That which does not kill us makes us stronger*, most certainly applies to sitting with our magical thinking, superstitions and obsessions, and not giving into them.

Magical thinking is inherent in many people's OCD. Magical thinking is the belief that actions have some magical quality or influence on things completely unrelated. For example, a person may believe things are okay as long as the shoes in her closet are aligned properly. Recently, a young woman told me if she always faced north, her family would be safe. She spent much of her time arranging her body parts to face this direction, oftentimes making her look bizarre to others.

There are hundreds of magical or superstitious beliefs underlying OCD. Are any of your beliefs magical? Write down your OCD fears and try to be objective, a mere observer of yourself. Evaluate whether or not your OCD fears are underscored by magical thoughts or beliefs, instead of rational ones. If they are, challenge them! Why would the magic apply to you and not others? Why do you have to take precautions and others do not. Nothing happens to them when they don't take these "preventative measures." Why is this?

If the problem can be solved, why worry?
If the problem cannot be solved, worrying will do you no good.
—Śāntideva

Stress

Stress is inevitable in life. We all have it and we all wish we didn't. However, it is not the stress of life that is the problem;

it is our **response** to it. When OCD is in the picture, stress can exacerbate obsessions and compulsions or it can revive OCD when it has been in remission. In times of stress, it is very important to remember to be strong with your OCD, while at the same time being compassionate with yourself, tending to your emotional needs. Remember, OCD provides a superficial feeling of being "in control" of life. It makes sense that when life becomes stressful OCD would "feel good," like it is somehow helping to put you back in control of your life. WRONG! OCD will slip back into control and your job is not to allow it back in the driver's seat. Remember, stress is a natural part of life; OCD is not.

Circling the Drain: Know your OCD triggers

Just as it is important to recognize when you are feeling stressed or out of control, it is also important to know your personal OCD triggers. When triggers are present, you can begin to "circle the drain" of OCD and can eventually, if you are not careful, get sucked down. Recently, Sheri and I were meeting to work on the book and she told me of a recent suicide that had occurred in her high-rise building. She noted the feelings of anxiety that followed (and persisted), as well as her increasing desire to fall back into old habits. She was circling her OCD drain. We talked about how her OCD was trying to reemerge by telling her maybe she was responsible for this terrible event. She recognized this event as a reminder of Jon's suicide and the painful feelings that still existed about his death. Most importantly, she was able to identify this trigger for what it was: a potential for relapse. She responded appropriately and took the necessary steps to take care of herself and not get sucked down the drain.

Ask yourself:
- What are your triggers?
- What makes you vulnerable to relapse?
- How can you respond when and if these events were to happen?

Life is messy!

I visited an out-of-town friend recently and noticed she was overly preoccupied with wiping crumbs off of the countertops. She was not able to sit through a meal without addressing the errant crumbs on the table. I watched her behavior for a few days and then had to ask: "What bothers you about the crumbs? What do you think would happen if those crumbs stayed there for the whole meal?" Interestingly, she had no answer. She reasoned aloud she was not disgusted by the crumbs, was not concerned about bugs being attracted to the crumbs; she was not concerned about contamination and she was not worried people would think badly of her if she had crumbs on the table. What was it then? In the end, she stated having no crumbs in her world was a metaphor for her life being in order. Somehow the crumbs symbolized the messiness of life. If she could remedy the messy crumbs, perhaps she might remedy the "messy" in her life. Sound familiar?

Although she probably does not have OCD, she engages in a common anxiety-reducing behavior. In the end we talked about how we all have to tolerate the messes of life. Crumbs are inherent in life and **that is okay**. She called me a few days after I left and reported she was leaving crumbs all over the kitchen and wiping them up after dinner. She felt like she was letting go of some of her need to "control the messes" of life.

Take a good look at your behavior(s) and what it (they) might be helping you feel better about. Maybe there is a bigger message in there that needs to be addressed. Maybe letting go of your need to control will be the key to freedom.

The Importance of Exercise

Exercise is something I like to call "mental health hygiene." Exercise has been found to help increase serotonin levels in the brain, and diminish feelings of anxiety and sadness. In addition, exercise can boost self-esteem, improve confidence and provide important social contact. In developing your plan for fighting OCD, (e.g., locating a therapist trained in ERP or reaching out to members of your family), remember to incorporate exercise into your routine. It does not need to be marathon training, but modest physical activity at least four times a week can significantly help your efforts. Even if you are not ready to do ERP, adding physical activity into your week can help set the stage for when you are ready to seek treatment.

CHAPTER 8
Maintaining Gains and Preventing Relapse

*Fortunately, I have developed a new understanding of
true control. I know that I can't predict or control what
will happen all the time because life is unpredictable.
But I can decide what my reactions will be.*

—From Panic to Power, Lucinda Bassett

Even as a person who regularly challenges her OCD and has
moved into "recovery," I still have to be careful. There are pulls
and nudges I regularly feel, and I have to be vigilant to ensure I
don't act on them. This next chapter explores how to successfully
move forward in your life, AFTER facing your OCD. How do
you keep from falling back into old behaviors? How do you
keep from letting OCD back in? How do you stay out of that
proverbial rabbit hole? The following are some suggestions that
worked for me.

Expect OCD Will Try to Reappear

OCD is an anxiety disorder, so it makes sense that when our stress levels rise, our need for that false sense of control grows stronger. It's important to note every time you give in to that little ritual or compulsion, you are reawakening the need for more and more rituals and ultimately, strengthening OCD. The moment you give in and check something, you are undoing some of the hard work you have done to be free of OCD.

Be Prepared

When I know a stressful situation is either upon me or imminently approaching, I emotionally and physically prepare myself. For example, when I know my husband is going out of town for a few days, I make sure I have a babysitter in place for a handful of hours each day; I'll move appointments to a different time to help me feel less stressed; I'll try to get to bed earlier; I'll try to stay away from the evening news; I'll make a point of doing yoga and deep breathing exercises every day while he is gone.

Yet as Suzanne talked about in the last chapter, there are times when life prevents us from planning and stress just crashes into our laps (e.g. We are exhausted, over-worked and emotional when we get the news someone we love suddenly passed away). When an emotional tsunami of stress comes our way, those pulls will most likely begin tugging at us full force. Like a recovering alcoholic, we may even fall off the OCD wagon. Ultimately however, whether we give in to one pull or one hundred, it is up to us to pick ourselves up and get back on the horse.

Case in point: we recently sold our home "spur of the moment" and needed to find a new place to live within two weeks' time. This occurred within the same time as the suicide in our building. And just following the suicide (yet prior to learning that we needed to be out of our unit pronto), Max and I had booked a last minute cruise with our family. So it was a matter of finding a home, moving in and hopping onto a ship all in little more than a fortnight! The pull to perform old rituals and compulsions was suddenly stronger than it had been in years. And I slipped…and slipped.

But something wonderful happened with all of my sudden "forced" exposures. I was experiencing a myriad of stressors yet simultaneously noting everything was okay. So slowly, after hitting a low point (a handful of days doing twenty plus minutes of rituals and compulsions), I started to challenge myself, AMIST all the external stress! I reminded myself of how far I'd come, and decided I wasn't going to allow an unfortunate death of a stranger or a sudden move and last minute getaway stop me from returning to my life of freedom. I stayed alert. I sat with pulls lower on my hierarchy and started to build confidence with each successful exposure. Not checking created a positive momentum for me and, before I knew it, I was actively seeking exposures once again. At first, my exposures were the forced, I-don't-have-a-choice kind (e.g. I can't find a pair of clean socks after the move, and we don't have a washing machine yet, so I'll **have to** "sit" knowing there are dirty socks on my feet). By deciding to see those naturally occurring exposures as a starting point to planned exposures; (e.g. I can use a *clean* towel now we have a washing machine, but I'm purposely going to use a *dirty* one to dry my face); by challenging myself in the face of adversity, I not only got out of the rabbit hole, but catapulted myself to an even stronger place than I was at the start of this book!

Something worth noting: never once did I berate myself for slipping. I learned early on with Morgan that "the inner critic" only exacerbates OCD. It is impossible to expect ourselves to climb up and out when we are feeling down and hopelessly caved in.

OCD is Tricky and Will Morph

As I've moved through my OCD hierarchy, I noticed one constant: OCD repeatedly and clandestinely alerts me to something new to worry about and check or do, (as Suzanne refers to it, the "Whack a Mole" phenomenon). For example, shortly before we moved, I sat with a strong desire to check that the fan in our bedroom was most definitely, positively off. I refused to check. Forty minutes later, my anxiety was much better. Unfortunately, while the pull to check the fan died, in its place was a sudden, overwhelming need to check that the nightlight in our bathroom wasn't touching the hand towel. My brain told me if I didn't check to confirm that the towel wasn't touching the nightlight then there could possibly be a fire. Again, insight clearly abandoned me here. It didn't matter that I already knew the nightlight's bulb wattage was next to nil. OCD was too busy filling my head with irrational fears. So I didn't check the fan, but ended up checking the nightlight. Fortunately, I was able to nip this new compulsion early on and am no longer checking the nightlight.

Know OCD will try to trick you; know it will morph into sudden new concerns, whispering you need to perform x, y, and z to be safe, healthy, etc. The key is to, as in the case of the nightlight, nip those new compulsions in the bud before they blossom into festering branches of doubt.

As Sheri describes so accurately, OCD does **not** want to die. When you are in the process of mastering your OCD, oftentimes it will morph or change in hopes of catching you off guard. Remember the metaphor of OCD as the fisherman and you are the fish? It is as if the fisherman is throwing different bait, a different flavor of juicy worm, hoping you will not recognize it and you will bite. Expect as you are moving forward, OCD will change and come at you disguised as a different concern. The answer is simply to recognize these pulls for what they are and ignore them. Eventually, OCD will become so weak it will give up. But OCD does not give up easily; so expect some morphing to occur before it eventually weakens to the point of dying.

Cognitive Errors that May Lead to Relapse

Earlier in this chapter we discussed cognitive errors common to OCD. In this section we will explore some cognitive errors often germane to general anxiety, but which can sabotage efforts to fight and master OCD. Think about these as more relevant to life, more relevant to relapse-prevention.

Discounting the Positive

If our perceptions create our reality, then it stands to reason that whatever we focus on grows. When I considered myself a failure with the bug incident, I'd never factored in all of the wonderful things I was doing: sitting with the exposure, looking forward to the day before me; challenging myself to rest next to the bug on the nightstand (When I very much wanted to leave the bed and flush the deceased insect down the toilet!) It's only after Morgan pointed out these accomplishments that my self-esteem, my inner strength and determination returned again.

I now see Morgan on a maintenance basis. She has provided me with cognitive and behavioral tools I regularly use to fight the "Doubting Disease." I am continually writing down the various cognitive errors in my judgment—catching myself faster with practice. No, it isn't easy, but it definitely works!

Each day, take a few minutes to write down what you *have done* as no accomplishment is too small. It is a strong antidote to the "Doubting Disease." Focusing on our successes, however small they may seem, sets a fertile foundation for more success.

When a person has moved into the relapse-prevention portion of treatment or what Sheri refers to as "maintenance," she is trying to maintain her treatment gains. At this stage, "slips" or minor setbacks will most likely occur, and it is helpful to expect they will. The most important thing is to keep a slip, a slip and not allow it to turn into a relapse. Changing the way you talk to yourself is a key to relapse-prevention. If you discount the positive and focus on the negative, you are treading very close to the perimeter of the rabbit hole, making it easy to fall back inside. For example, I had a patient who had not checked the stove in weeks. She was so proud of herself and was on the road to recovery. One morning, she was feeling uncertain and checked the stove. After saying a few self-berating statements like: "Why the heck did you do that? You are a failure! You screwed up," she moved into perspective and reminded herself it was only one check and considered what was different about today; why did this happen now? Upon reflection, she remembered that she was awaiting the results of her husband's recent biopsy, and this had caused her to feel frightened and uncertain about the future. It made sense to her she was hungry for that feeling of control (albeit superficial and deceptive). By looking within, she was suddenly in problem-solving mode, thereby allowing her slip to remain a slip.

Look at slips as opportunities to learn about yourself. Ask yourself: *What happened? Why did I do that ritual? What do I need to do differently next time?* Keep in mind all of the progress you have made; view slips as opportunities to learn about yourself and, more importantly, keep in mind how to avoid making the same mistake in the future.

Catastrophic Thinking

Since those of us with OCD tend to obsess and perform compulsive actions without any rational basis; since we naturally possess an affinity for doubt, it is no surprise one of our pitfalls is catastrophic thinking. This is one of those cognitive errors I almost always need to make note of in order to excavate myself mentally from the rabbit hole.

Here's an example from one of my earlier catastrophic thinking moments:

My father called. What if I get pulled into the abusive cycle again? What if the "Man Upstairs" thinks I've let Him down by not having a continued relationship with my father? What if I'm up all night thinking about this? What if I can no longer function in life because the guilt eats away at me?

You could argue the excerpt above (an actual sample from a "homework" assignment that Morgan gave me years ago) is not only providing examples of catastrophic thinking but also fortune telling and discounting the positive. Many of the cognitive errors in this chapter overlap, twisting in our minds and preventing any positive thoughts from getting in there and taking root. Morgan's assignment was to write down my fears—a powerful way to literally face them—and then identify the cognitive errors in my thinking. And the final step? I needed to write down alternate, healthier thoughts. I remember shaking as I made my list of rational arguments to fight the all-encompassing fear. Here's what I wrote:

My parents ripped up their parent cards years ago when they first began to abuse me.
I am too strong to get pulled back into my nuclear family's toxic cycle of abuse.
There is no room for guilt—no space or place for it because I haven't done anything wrong to either my father or mother.
My parents speak of love but have no understanding of it.
Nothing has changed: my father is still an abuser and I am still a free WOMAN—no longer the little girl he sees me as.
My father's pain is his own; his issues were brought about by himself.
I am free of guilt.

I deserve to be angry at my parents' pathetic attempt at reconciliation: three years and all my father makes is one lousy phone call to me?

Big deal! To have a relationship of any kind would destroy my soul and by extension, my new, loving, centered family.

I am a beautiful sleeper and one lousy, self-centered phone call from my father doesn't change this fact.

Here are my feelings after this particular cognitive exercise:

Empowered,

determined,

angry (at my parents),

free,

centered,

capable,

mature,

wise,

independent,

relaxed.

Morgan referred to this particular assignment as a cognitive log. It is one of my favorite tools to get me out of crisis mode. I can't recommend it enough! Please don't let the formality of the term deter you: a cognitive log merely involves a pen and paper. Since OCD is the "Doubting Disease," we need all the help we can get to think rationally. The cognitive log offers us a simple (albeit, not always easy!) tool to dig ourselves back out of the circuitous rabbit hole. To recap, here are the four key steps:

1. Identify your fear or source of anxiety.
2. Identify what cognitive errors are germane to the said fear/anxiety (i.e. black and white thinking, fortune telling, unfair comparisons, etc.)

3. List alternate, rational thoughts.
4. Describe how you feel after step #3.

Unfair Comparisons

Oh how anxiety loves to play the unfair comparison card! For a few weeks I was exhausted, utterly drained and feeling like even small things (e.g. a shower) were a great effort. It didn't help that my brain regularly noted other mothers who looked perky and pretty, energetic and up for anything. *That mother has two more kids than you do, and she is always well-dressed and in a great mood. What's your excuse, Sheri? And that mother has two kids just like you, but somehow she manages to create book after book. Why does it take you so long to produce a manuscript? That mother attends yoga five days a week; why can't you make it to the gym more than once a week?*

If I let anxiety's unfair comparisons percolate in my head without a fight, my self-esteem would be hanging by a gossamer thread! And as we know, low self-esteem is the precursor to a stronger bully. So I took out my journal and wrote down what was going on in *my* life—no one else's:

I am tired because I spend hours each week at the doctor for our youngest son who seems to catch everything from strep to bacterial infections in the intestines!

I am tired because my husband is starting a brand new business and is hardly ever home these days.

I am tired because we just moved.

I am tired because I was diagnosed with both strep and a massive sinus infection.

I am tired because I am pursuing my passion for writing while raising two beautiful boys.

I am tired because our dog was up vomiting last night.

I am tired because my body requires a certain amount of sleep I am just not able to get at this moment in time.

I learned sometime later that the exercise fanatic with the beautiful body considers yoga her Prozac and regularly fights clinical depression; the mother who is always perky and energetic isn't happy with the man she married; the prolific author with young kids doesn't make time for friends.

It is impossible to walk in someone else's shoes, so why try? We need to walk in our own shoes—be they worn sneakers or high heels. Only we know what they feel like; only we know what we can and cannot tolerate. When we try to slip into someone else's shoes we become vulnerable to stress and potential relapse. Comparing ourselves to others causes us to question ourselves and through unfair comparisons, makes us feel less worthy.

Social comparison always leads to suffering. Usually, people compare themselves in the negative direction to people whom they perceive to be somehow "better." These comparisons lead to feelings of worthlessness, sadness, inferiority and a desire to have things others have. Interestingly, research has shown even the upward comparisons (where you perceive yourself somehow better than another person) lead to feelings of guilt and frustration. Either way, it is a losing prospect. Although social comparison is unrelated to OCD, it is important to remember it *is* related to anxiety and how one feels about oneself. For this reason, it is important because **when you feel more anxious, you are vulnerable to stress, anxiety and potential relapse.**

131

Mind Reading

I once watched a short film in college that showed a close up of a man's face against a blank background. His face was without expression. The film went on to show horrific events taking place in the man's life: bombs exploding, planes tunneling to the ground, young children screaming out in pain and fear. The background changed again showing violins playing, flowers blooming and ice-cream. Our professor asked what we saw in the man's face throughout the film. We noted he grew sad when the background changed from a blank canvas to a landscape of war and his expression morphed again to one of vulnerable kindness when there were violins and flowers in the background. Some of the other students' comments described the man's original expression as cold and distant, the second expression as fierce and somewhat cruel; the third expression was seen as calm, but wistful.

The professor gave our class a cryptic smile and said, "The man's expression never changed."

So what had happened? How could we students have felt so confident we knew what the man in the film was feeling? According to the professor, we were subconsciously taking in the background images and projecting how we might feel onto the expressionless face of the actor! We were essentially mind reading!

To a certain extent, we all need to read expressions and body language to survive socially. But there's a fine, yet distinct, line between understanding social cues, (e.g. a nod of the head means hello; a wave of the hand means goodbye) and reading *into* them. (e.g. Why the quick nod of her head at me? Is she mad at me? Did I offend her?) And when your bully is OCD, allowing yourself to go for a ride on the Mind Reading Train can lead to a one way ticket down the rabbit hole.

Here's another fact: short of being psychic, you will never know what others are truly thinking or why they do the things they do.

Those of us with the "Doubting Disease" typically don't make the best mind readers as we are more likely to project our fears onto others without considering alternate possibilities for their behavior that have nothing whatsoever to do with us. So accept your shortcomings in this area and focus on what IS in your power: living your *own* life, one independent of others' inexplicable behaviors. Your mind and heart will thank you for it!

Personalization

Personalizing and mind reading go hand in hand. Personalizing is the act of taking another's actions and assuming they are directly related to you.

Here's an example of personalization that happened to me a good year ago. I was on the road, idling at a stoplight when I noticed my friend pull up in her car right beside me. I began to wave and call her name.

"Hey, Susan! How funny we bumped into each other like this!"

Susan, a normally warm person, turned to me and gave me a tight smile before frowning and looking away. The light turned green and she sped off.

It would have been easy for me to assume the worst: *her birthday is tomorrow; did she think I'd forgotten and didn't care? She probably thinks I'm a selfish person. Or maybe it's because she thought*

133

I appeared too eager to see her, waving my hand in the air like a five year old over-dosed on sugar. After all, it is a relatively new friendship. Maybe I scared her away now...

The above thoughts swarmed in my head, but I refused to let myself be mentally bitten up by them. I called her later that night and asked if she was okay, mentioning that she seemed a bit upset on the road today. It turns out she had just walked away from a major fight with her husband and was holding back her tears when I happened to see her.

So it was clear: I was not the cause of Susan's unfriendly expression—this time. **Here's the important lesson: most things aren't personal. Whether we receive compliments or insults, neither one should have power over us or how we feel about ourselves.**

When I severed the relationship with my parents, I received a fair amount of negative feedback from well-meaning, but ignorant strangers: "But they're your parents. I don't understand how you can just walk away from them," or "It's a commandment to honor your father and mother. You are breaking a sacred commandment."

Ultimately, I couldn't take the above comments personally. I needed to do what was good *for me*, not for them. It didn't matter *they* didn't understand; what mattered was *I* understood. Learning not to take what others say and do personally is necessary, not only for extinguishing the flames of OCD, but for a life filled with inner peace. If you spend your life running to everyone for validation, you'll never get everyone to agree; you'll never learn to listen to your own voice.

When you commit to not taking things personally, you put yourself back in the driver's seat of your own life.

Listening to Old Tapes

Insanity: doing the same thing over and over again and expecting different results.

—Albert Einstein

We all have an inner mental tape. It regularly tells us what we think about ourselves and the world around us. Most messages are formed in our early years when we are impressionable and essentially a blank canvas. Often these messages play unconsciously, our inner tapes streaming soundlessly through our psyches. Since our thoughts possess the power to create our reality, it seems in our best interest to examine those messages and bring them in to our conscious awareness. In order to master OCD, it is vital for me to draw those dormant messages into the light regularly, to take an honest look at them and determine which ones are helpful and which ones need to be kicked to the curb.

Chances are if you have OCD, you struggle with a myriad of doubts and fears. Earlier in this book, Suzanne and I wrote about the importance of recognizing your particular fear(s) and the subsequent rituals and compulsions that follow. Now it's time to excavate your psyche even further by identifying what you think about yourself and life itself. Below is brief list of my old inner tapes:

I am a selfish person.

I am an irresponsible person.

I am too sensitive for this world.

Everyone is only out for himself.

Deep down, I am not a good, trustworthy person.

I strongly suggest you take a good week to consider your inner tapes and WRITE DOWN those insidious messages. We can't expect to change our tapes if we can't identify them. Writing down our inner tapes brings them into the light, into our *conscious* minds.

Once you have identified your inner tapes, it's time to consider them. Are some of them worth keeping? In my case, most were overdue for the trash bin. I kept the ones I liked and got to work on erasing the ones I didn't want. The key is to change each negative tape to an accurate, loving statement about yourself and your perceptions of life. Here's what my new list looks like:

I am a thoughtful person who gives to others, but also makes time for myself.

I am a very responsible person.

My sensitivity is a gift to myself and others.

Everyone in this life wants love.

I am a good person.

I am worthy of love.

Here's where the tough work comes in: taking the time to change your tapes. The tape I struggled with the most was "I am a good person"—most likely because my father devoted a great portion of my early years telling me to "rot in hell." At first, I couldn't even say the words "I am a good person" without rolling my eyes and uncomfortably laughing. Over time and with great repetition, I practiced replacing the old tapes with the new ones (by saying the new tapes to myself and aloud), and slowly these old tapes began to vanish. Years later, I am able to look in the mirror and tell my reflection, "I am a good person" with sincerity and compassion. It was hard work, but I am no longer questioning my worth or my heart. Changing my inner tapes eradicated a great wall of doubt. I now live a life of psychological freedom. I want this for you.

Investing the time to examine your inner tapes or beliefs about yourself will help you to grow stronger, to know yourself (your strengths and liabilities), and to have a true, honest perspective of your life. Being strong and knowing yourself can bolster your defenses against stress, anxiety and the OCD bully.

Setting Unrealistic Expectations

So here I am, down to about five minutes of rituals and compulsions a day, regularly challenging myself to sit with new pulls, when suddenly, I find myself spending an hour checking the fan in our bedroom!

What happened?

The next morning, exhausted and emotionally letting an old tape, ("I am a failure") sneak its way back into my psyche, I told my husband what happened.

"Sheri, you just stopped talking to your sister for the first time in your life. Yesterday was her birthday. Give yourself a break."

Oh, that….Yes, after years of watching my sister continue to accept our abusive parents into her life, I made the decision to keep my distance, albeit temporarily, from her. Watching her suffer was too much for me. Forty-eight hours later, on my sister's birthday, I wasn't thinking about my sister, I was suddenly obsessed with the fan above our bed falling from the ceiling and crashing on us as we slept.

When you have OCD, your mind constantly reaches for things to control—often in an effort to feel better about the things in life that we can't control (e.g. a recently severed relationship between siblings). When our stress levels rise, our desire to control that uncomfortable feeling shoots up, too.

My husband helped me understand why I suddenly felt urges to ritualize, and as a result, I was able to get some much-needed perspective. I spoke kindly to myself, recognizing I wasn't a failure but a woman in mourning for her sister. It was unrealistic for me (in light of the recent circumstances) to expect to have a normal day of five minutes' worth of compulsions.

By facing the real situation (mourning the loss of the relationship with my sister), I was able to return to challenging my OCD and ultimately, face my pain. Accept and honor your feelings; don't try to control them superficially. Know some times are going to be harder than others. By appreciating our circumstances, we become better at recognizing our true feelings and forgo trying to run away from them through unnecessary rituals.

"The unexamined life is not worth living."

—Socrates

Becoming Your Own Therapist

When you are moving into "maintenance" or "relapse prevention" you ultimately must become your own therapist. OCD is not going away; it may be much better now, but you are always at risk for its return. So you have to become your own therapist, know its stealthy nature and presume it will at least attempt to revisit you. One of the most important pieces of relapse prevention treatment is to think of exposures as *opportunities*. This may sound ridiculous, but it works.

In the chapter, *Getting to Work*, we explored naturally occurring exposures, and when it comes to relapse-prevention they are critical. Unplanned exposures, things that just come up in life, are wonderful opportunities to face your fears. Be on the lookout for OCD to sneak back into your calmer, more balanced life. Know it for what it is, and refuse to listen when it whispers scary things to you. In fact, it may be helpful to think of "doing the opposite" as the knee-jerk reaction to OCD. When OCD tells you to do something, do the opposite. If OCD tells you to check, don't check; if OCD tells you to wash, don't wash; if OCD tells you to go back and see, keep going. Ultimately, you are the only person in the world who can master OCD, and the way to master is by not listening.

Seek Out Exposures

One idea is to approach your day actually looking for things to spike your anxiety. This involves taking the unplanned or naturally occurring exposures one step further. Not only are there naturally occurring exposures all around you, but you are *deliberately* going to seek them out! Instead of thinking of exposures as horrible things you must face, think of them as opportunities to expedite getting well and staying well. Examples of this might include:

1. Carry a contaminated paper towel with you in your pocket or purse. Every time you wash your hands, re-contaminate them.
2. Drive down a bumpy road and remind yourself you might be hitting innocent people all along the way.
3. Make mistakes while you pray.
4. Press send on an email you know has errors.
5. Eat at a restaurant you feel is dirty or contaminated.

In order to become your own therapist, you must know the process of fighting OCD. Here is what you need to remember:

1. Know your OCD themes and your obsessional fears.
2. Refuse to listen to your OCD and do not do what it tells you to do.

1. Expect OCD will morph, tempting you to fear new and different things.
2. Expect OCD to try randomly to get you to "bite."
3. Whether it is a brand new or old ritual from years ago, **do the opposite of whatever OCD tells you to do**.
4. Continue with exposures and ritual prevention **for life**.

If you think of fighting OCD as a process, like weight management or living a healthy / active lifestyle, it becomes easier to tolerate the long-term commitment. Think about having an OCD bank account. Each day you are putting a few dollars into your account. You do this by facing exposures, not doing rituals and welcoming anxiety-producing situations. Each day, even if you only contribute a few cents, you are at least going in the right direction. If you *do* ritualize, you are making a withdrawal from your account. This means you must go back to contributing. Over time, your goal is to accumulate a large "savings" of confidence, strength and psychological flexibility (the ability to tolerate a variety of situations). Our goal is to make you a psychologically wealthy person!

In the next chapter, we will highlight the importance of acceptance and taking responsibility in this process. Acceptance is a mental attitude about having OCD and this greatly effects how you face it. Acceptance is critical in the process of fighting OCD over the lifespan. Responsibility means knowing it is up to you to make changes in your life. The question is: Are you ready?

CHAPTER 9
Your Wake Up Call: Facing the Queen of Hearts

Having Zoe saved my life. It was my wake-up call. There were so many things I didn't want to pass on to her.

—Lisa Bonet

If you do what you've always done, you'll get what you've always gotten.

—Anthony Robbins

I can't emphasize enough both the importance and the **necessity** of regular exposure in order to master OCD. Writing this book with Suzanne has been its own form of exposure work for me and, as a result, I am that much more empowered to sit with those pulls. I am shortly about to create an exposure by disclosing another harrowing personal anecdote.

If you've followed this book from the first page, you know for years I did everything BUT sit with my anxiety. I had a brief attachment to sleeping pills, adopted a boatload of needless rituals and developed a penchant for staying busy—all in the hopeless attempt to avoid dealing with my OCD. I secretly performed these rituals and compulsions over a period of years. I would rationalize and tell myself, "It's not like my 'little checks' and prayers are hurting anyone," and "It's not like I'm an alcoholic or drug addict. I'm a functioning adult who needs to check and move things here and there to feel better—big deal," and "My OCD actually *helps* me. It keeps me super-responsible and prevents me from thinking about unpleasant things."

OCD is a liar; OCD is the enemy; OCD might begin as a subtle whisper to check, wash, pray, etc., but once you do what that voice tells you to do, it grows into an unrelenting monster and renders you its prisoner. OCD is a sinister stranger offering you candy with a diabetic smile. If you take the "candy" you are only going to wind up sick.

Still, everyone needs to find his/her own wake up call. Suzanne and I offer countless analogies to describe the tenacious misfiring in our OCD-wired brains; we can pontificate on the necessity of sitting with your exposures until the figurative cows come home, but our words only have the potential to help when we are ready and able to listen.

My wake-up call came when I was pregnant with our second child. I was halfway through the second trimester when I began having contractions. The doctor put me on bed rest. Back then I was seeing a wonderful therapist who helped me understand and come to terms with my past. But all the talk therapy in the world can't contend with or diminish OCD. So I continued to perform an ever-increasing amount of rituals. OCD is an all-consuming beast: the more you feed it, the hungrier it gets, demanding ever-more "food" with time.

At the time of my doctor's strict orders for bed rest, I'd been following OCD's demand to check under the bed. Not having begun any CBT work and without the tools to fight OCD, I felt powerless to the monstrous command to check under our bed. It was my kneeling on all fours, with premature contractions to check, check and re-check under our bed that was my sobering wake up call. I remember the growing weight of our son inside of me and the desperate panic I felt to check, regardless of the consequences to my son. Tears streamed down my cheeks as I checked under our bed as if there were a gun to my head. It was awful. It was terrifying. It was unthinkable.

No longer could I rationalize that the OCD wasn't affecting others. Our precious unborn child's welfare was put at risk each time I checked! It was unacceptable; I needed help. That shameful, horrific moment was the start of my recovery from OCD, the spark that fueled my desire to eradicate the endless torment of OCD from my life, forever.

I hope that my story is the only wake-up call you need. Don't continue to let OCD take over your life like I did. First, consider the ways OCD impacts your life, how it prevents you from enjoying yourself or, as in my case, how it can negatively affect the people you love the most. Just as there is no such thing as a "little pregnant," there is no such thing as a "little check." Don't wait until you are so deep down the rabbit hole you no longer know up from down, right from wrong. Remember, OCD is the "Doubting Disease." Its goal is to make you doubt everything and, consequently, follow its every command. By recognizing how OCD negatively impacts your life, you can move toward action; toward a refusal to heed the bully's commands; toward accepting doubt as inherent in both OCD and life.

Take a minute to write down how OCD impacts your life. Does it take up time? Does it prevent you from being close to the people you love? Does it prevent you from feeling happy? Does it govern your every move? By writing down the burden-like effects of OCD, you are creating mental ammunition for combating it.

Taking Responsibility

When you blame others, you give up your power to change.
—Author Unknown

You must take personal responsibility. You cannot change the circumstances, the seasons, or the wind, but you can change yourself.
—Jim Rohn

I grew up in an abusive home and that abuse continued until I severed the relationship with my parents. I was a widow at twenty-five after the horrific suicide of my young husband. I have OCD. I can choose to focus on the tragedies in my life or I can take these circumstances, learn from them and move forward. Remember, what we focus on grows. I much prefer to cultivate gratitude for life.

My son's karate teacher has a saying: "Excuses are like armpits: everyone has a couple and they always stink." We can all find excuses in our lives not to fight OCD:

It's too hard.

I'm worried about: "fill-in-the-blank."

When the situation changes, I will try to sit with my exposures.

It's just not a good time to have to deal with all that anxiety.

I'm terrified.

My "fill-in-the-blank relative" isn't supportive.

I have OCD because of bad genes. End of story.

Excuses and blame are a waste of your energy and time. They keep OCD in the driver's seat and relegate you to being a passenger in the car of your own life. It's taking responsibility that empowers us and gives us the inner strength we need to master the insidious misfiring of our brains. Wallowing in self-pity and negativity is a waste of time and energy and will not lead to healing, ever. Believe me, I know because I have lived it. Whenever I fall off of the proverbial wagon and give into a pull to check the stove is off, putting myself down only increases my doubt. "Did I check? Let me just make sure." Needing to check *again*, it becomes almost second nature to feel bad about myself. It is not until I make a point of resisting further checks and giving myself a much-needed pep talk that I can excavate my psyche out of the insatiable darkness. It is that internal dialogue which greatly determines how long and deep my stay in the rabbit hole will be.

I strongly recommend you take a moment to write down your excuses for not sitting with your exposures. Then write a list of positive, encouraging statements right beside those weak excuses. Here's what my list looks like:

It's too hard! Yes, fighting OCD is extremely hard. But I prefer to always fight it than feed it. Each time I conquer OCD, I take back real control.

I am worried about moving. So we might be moving again; the only constant is change. There will never be a good time to sit with exposures; life is organic and busy.

When the situation changes, I will deal with my OCD. It will never be a good time to face my anxiety; now is as good a time as any!

I'm terrified! So I'm terrified. I'd rather face my fears than sit with a false sense of control. On the other side of every fear is freedom; I choose freedom.

My parents aren't supportive. My biological family doesn't respect my decision to go for therapy. That is their choice as it is my choice to continue going to Morgan to help keep OCD from returning to a clinical level. I cannot control what others think. I can only control my own actions.

I have OCD because of bad genes, end of story. I know of at least two biological family members with OCD. So there is clearly a genetic component to my OCD, but this doesn't mean that I can't get better, that I can't master my OCD.

Morgan often compares OCD to diabetes. Both are highly treatable conditions that are managed with lifestyle changes. Both sometimes require medication. While diabetics often need to change their diet and fitness routine, individuals diagnosed with OCD often need specific tools to help get them and keep them out of the clinically significant realm. Both depend on the patient taking responsibility and working hard for successful treatment to occur.

Bottom line: you can read all the self-help books on OCD you like and find the best psychologist who specializes in OCD, but none of it will help until you are ready to take responsibility for your life, commit to sitting with your anxiety, and resist doing your rituals.

Motivation

Do not wait to strike till the iron is hot; but make it hot by striking.
—William B. Sprague

Nothing contributes so much to tranquilize the mind as a steady purpose—a point on which the soul may fix its intellectual eye.
—Mary Shelley

Nothing great was ever achieved without enthusiasm.
—Ralph Waldo Emerson

Knowing that treating OCD involves regular vigilance, knowing that the misfiring in our brains may quiet down with behavior therapy, but that it will never completely disappear, it is necessary to find motivation in order to challenge continuously our pulls and insatiable appetites for false control. What motivates you can look very different from what motivates me. And what motivates you today may not motivate you tomorrow. Since relapse prevention and living a life with little interruption from OCD is our goal, it is important to find a spark or some source of inspiration to keep us resisting those nudging whispers to check, pray, ritualize, touch—whatever our bullies tell us to do.

The following are some motivators that work for me. I encourage you to use the ones that help and discard the ones that don't "move" you in some way to challenge yourself. It is also a good idea to come up with your own motivators. The best fuel for change is often self-created.

Tokens

One of my compulsions is an overwhelming pull to confess things to my husband. I am not referring to the things one *should* disclose to her spouse, e.g., "I'm having an affair with our plumber." The pull I feel to confess involves petty and trivial information that doesn't have any effect on my husband or anyone else for that matter.

Case in point: the other night I told my husband we were out of raspberries. But when we got home, I noticed there were, in fact, raspberries still in our fridge. It didn't matter I truly believed there weren't any raspberries in the fridge; my OCD started whispering I needed to confess to my husband and let him know I was wrong, that there was in fact a perfectly full pint of raspberries ready for consumption in our fridge.

Morgan suggested I use tokens to control my desire to confess. At the start of the week I would allot myself a specified number of tokens. Each time I confessed, I would have to "pay" a token to my husband. The goal is never to go over the allotment of tokens in a given week. I started with seven tokens, one for each day of the week. I am currently down to having only four tokens a week at my disposal. If I can go an entire week without using one token, I treat myself to something. But if I use even one token, I don't allow myself to enjoy whatever treat I'd planned for myself. As I write this, the week is almost over and I've already spent one token confessing about those raspberries. I had planned to treat myself to a yummy massage, but this will have to wait until next week.

My husband loves the token system. Before the token system, I would easily waste his time and mine with a good 15-20 minutes each day of unnecessary confessions. It is empowering to sit with my pull to confess and enjoy those extra 100+ minutes instead. And the longer I go without "spending" my tokens, the more independent I become.

Experiment with the token system. When I first started it, I gave myself a treat if I managed to go the entire week and didn't fall into a negative balance; then with time, I increased the stakes, allowing myself a treat only if I had at least one unspent token. It is only recently that I am super stringent and only allow myself a treat if I didn't use one single token. Keep increasing the stakes. Remember OCD dies when we are more and more willing to feel uncomfortable; the more we challenge ourselves, the more likely we are to defeat OCD.

We are always getting ready to live, but never living.
—**Ralph Waldo Emerson**

Readiness for Change

Sheri has eloquently described the ingredients of taking responsibility and motivation. Both are required for the recipe of OCD treatment. Another key ingredient, perhaps the most important of all is readiness for change. As with any behavioral change, whether it is weight loss, quitting smoking or giving up alcohol, one must be ready. I can take responsibility for my smoking by knowing I must make change; I can be motivated by purchasing nicotine replacement therapies; but, I must be *ready* actually to implement a smoking cessation plan for change to occur. Readiness involves a willingness to:

1. change how you do things;
2. implement strategies that are new and different (and sometimes contrary to what we think is right); and
3. suffer a bit in the process.

This last one is the hardest one to swallow. OCD treatment is hard and requires a bit of suffering. If you feel like you are motivated to face your OCD and wonder if you are ready, ask yourself these questions:
- Is now the right time for me?
- Do I have the energy and time to commit to this right now?
- Am I willing to experience some anxiety (sometimes intense anxiety) in order to be successful?
- Do I have the support I need from those around me?
- Am I willing to change my routine and how I approach my day?
- Have I identified a trained therapist to help me in this process?

149

If, after answering these questions, you feel like you are at the point of readiness then we suggest you move forward. If you have reservations about the process of change and whether or not you are at the point of readiness, that **is** okay. We feel it would be better for you to digest the information in this book and to continue with your education about OCD and OCD treatment until you have the time, energy, support and knowledge to move forward. Be careful not to beat yourself up for not moving forward at this time, because you may be ready in the coming weeks, months or years. We would rather you wait and experience success, as opposed to pushing forward before you are ready and possibly experiencing failure. In this next section, Sheri talks about some specific ways she encouraged herself along the way.

Penning a Letter from Your Highest Self

Take a moment to look back at your OCD hierarchy. What gets your OCD bullying at full force? What are the exposures most difficult for you? Each of us with OCD has at least one Achilles' heel. When we face head-on whatever fear plagues us, our fear grows smaller because we are taking action.

One of my Achilles' heels is anticipatory anxiety—particularly on nights prior to those early mornings, when I know I have a lot of responsibility on my plate for the upcoming day. Having two school-aged children, I know early mornings are more the norm than the exception, so my exposure is pretty constant, allowing my anxiety to go way down—as long as I get to bed at a reasonable time.

However, there is often so much to do during the day that I end up working into the evening (e.g. email, laundry, bills, writing assignments, etc.); by the time I make it to bed it is after midnight and that's when OCD begins to bully me. After a few late nights, I can easily become frazzled, thereby allowing OCD back in the driver's seat of my life. That's when I pen myself a letter. I compose them in the morning, typically after an evening of checking, when the night's exhaustion and panic are still fresh in my memory. Once I get going with my day, and drink a strong cup of java, I am less anxious, less concerned about my OCD fears. Unfortunately, once evening approaches, my doubts and obsessions begin to fester once again. So morning letters to myself are key. Below is an excerpt from a morning letter written in my journal over a year ago:

Dear P.M. Sheri,
Lights out by 10 P.M. tonight! This is A.M. Sheri, the woman who pays for your late night Internet roaming and novel reading.
Last night, you sat with the anxiety of not knowing if the oven was off. True, you sat with it for an hour, but then you panicked because by that time it was close to 1:30 A.M.! This panic led to more rituals and an even later bedtime. Think of how good you'd feel going to bed two hours earlier. Tonight, go to bed early and avoid all of this unnecessary drama. I will thank you in the morning.
Also, I'm proud of you for not seeking reassurance from Max tonight. Keep it up!
Love,
Your Highest Self

I read this letter to myself each night for the next week, which helped me make different decisions at night to get to bed earlier. Just as a diabetic needs to alter her diet to combat the insulin disorder, I need to get myself to bed by 10 P.M. regularly in order to prevent a relapse of OCD. I also needed to encourage myself in a kind and nurturing way. Being a strong support to yourself throughout this process will help you feel less beaten down and discouraged.

The letter from your highest self, written when you are feeling positive and rational, is a great motivator for challenging OCD because you are writing to yourself when you are not experiencing anxiety; thus you are in a great place to argue with that "irrational" self. I often think of it as a letter to my childhood self, the one who was lying in bed terrified she could not sleep, obsessed with shadows and strange noises; a letter encouraging that young Sheri to grow up and not be afraid anymore.

Audio Record Yourself

I typically find it is easier to resist OCD's whispers after a session of CBT work with Morgan. However, while having a supportive therapist in your life can prove helpful, especially in the beginning, depending solely on one is both unrealistic and counter-productive for the long-term. When I first began challenging OCD with Cognitive Behavior Therapy, I would often express to Morgan how quickly my sense of empowerment would contort into shaky fear once I was by myself. I wanted to bring my wonderful therapist home and have her walk through my fears. I wanted her reassurance I could ignore those visceral pulls to check and ritualize.

Being the good CBT therapist she is, and knowing reassuring me was not in my best interest, Morgan suggested a healthier alternative: a tape recording of herself verbally walking me through my nighttime exposures. Let me be clear, her message to me was I was strong enough to handle the exposures, not reassuring me I was safe.

Listening to Morgan's calm, direct voice definitely helped me give up a handful of rituals and compulsions. But it was her suggestion I tape record my *own* voice that had an even bigger impact on me. Tape recording yourself is the auditory equivalent to penning a letter from your Highest Self: both involve taking action, which is key to mastering OCD; both are solid tools to getting you back in the driver's seat of your life; both require self-awareness that fosters a strong sense of empowerment; and, most importantly, both are supportive, nurturing adjuncts to ERP that keep motivation and morale high during times of strife and struggle.

It is surreal and oddly comforting to hear your own voice guide you out of the land of doubt and into a world of rational confidence. No matter how wonderful your therapist may be, she is not you. She can cheer you on as you climb Mt. Everest, but ultimately, it's your feet determining whether you reach the top or trip on a figurative rock. Ultimately, mastering and keeping OCD at bay is up to you and your willingness to both internalize and utilize what you learn in therapy. If we can find comfort and encouragement in our own voice, we can keep our feet firmly planted on the top of the mountain, far away from the bottomless pit of doubt.

Find a Support Group or Mentor

Friends are angels who lift our feet when our
own wings have trouble remembering how to fly.
—Author Unknown

As empowered and independent as I am today, I would most likely still be diagnosed with OCD, without support from my husband and therapist. Morgan provided me with the necessary

OUT OF THE RABBIT HOLE

cognitive tools and both she and Max encouraged me to sit through the behavioral component of challenging OCD. Both are nurturing yet firm, challenging me to do harder and harder tasks along the way. They are my personal behavioral trainers, my cheerleaders rooting for me to search out exposures and not engage in needless rituals, even when I still have pulls to do so.

I have reached a point where I no longer feel a need to visit weekly with Morgan and it's rare for me to seek reassurance from my husband. I stand proudly at the top of my OCD Mountain, knowing I don't need Morgan or Max to negotiate successfully this life of newfound freedom. I never would have even attempted the climb without having a support system in place, ready to catch me if (and I did—many times!) I fell.

Who is in *your* support system? Are they prepared to help you through your journey? Have you sought help from people in the OCD community through the IOCDF (www.ocfoundation.org) and local OCD support groups? Look around and consider what help is available to you. **Ask for help.** You may be surprised to discover how willing people are to help and support you.

Our book demonstrates what successful treatment looks like, but walking through your own personal shadow of doubt requires a determination that is best fueled by a supportive friend, therapist or family member. Maybe you need all three. Maybe you only need one. But just as a recovering alcoholic needs a sponsor to get her through those tough days, your chances of mastering OCD increase when you know someone is on your side, providing the emotional support you need through this difficult process.

When we know someone is there for us, rooting for us to challenge OCD, there is also accountability. Part of my reluctance to end therapy with Morgan is because I know each time I see her, I'm expected to account for my latest exposure work. Additionally, when I feel a pull to check something, there is my husband, clearing his throat—an unspoken signal to sit back down and not touch, check or move anything.

As Suzanne mentioned in **Readiness for Change**, I also strongly recommend waiting to challenge yourself until you have a solid, nurturing and informed (regarding treatment for OCD) support system in place.

How Family Can Help

Being a family member of a person with OCD is tremendously difficult for a variety of reasons. Whether it be a parent, a spouse or a sibling, watching a loved one suffer with fears and rituals (which the family member knows are irrational) can be frustrating, to say the least. In addition, family members are often asked to participate in the OCD rituals, e.g., washing their hands even though they are not dirty, putting objects in a certain order to satisfy their loved one, reassuring their loved one that something is "okay" or checking doors and windows to relax their partner. Many times family members reluctantly participate in these rituals just to "keep the peace."

There are some wonderful books written for family members of people with OCD (*Obsessive Compulsive Disorder: A Survival Guide For Family And Friends*, by Roy C., *Loving Someone with OCD: Help for You and Your Family*, by Karen J. Landsman and *Obsessive Compulsive Disorder: New Help for the Family*, by Herbert L. Gravitz) and this section is in no way attempting to replace that literature. However, it is important to acknowledge how OCD affects not only the person suffering with the disorder, but also the loved ones who surround them. Family members can be instrumental in supporting you to accept OCD is an issue; to help you identify a trained therapist who can provide appropriate treatment (ERP), and to validate how hard therapy for OCD can be.

During therapeutic work, the therapist may ask family members to resist engaging in rituals, despite your insistence to do them. **This intervention is best done with the guidance of a therapist**. Sometimes family members attempt to be helpful by refusing to engage in or enable rituals prematurely, before you are ready. While ultimately this may be what is best, if it is done prematurely and without your consent, it can backfire, causing feelings of frustration, hopelessness and a perceived lack of support. When family members are more motivated than their loved one for treatment, it can create feelings of pressure and even anger, causing the individual to lose invaluable motivation to change.

If you are not yet in therapy and are still just considering getting help for your OCD, it may be time to garner support from those who love you. Maybe you have not told your loved ones you have OCD for fear that they would judge you. Admitting to loved ones (whom you trust) that you struggle with OCD is an important first step. Help family members to understand what OCD is and why it is very hard for you to change your behavior. This process will empower you and help to reduce any shame associated with OCD.

CHAPTER 10
Out of the Rabbit Hole

I can't go back to yesterday because I was a different person then.
— *Alice's Adventures in Wonderland,* **Lewis Carroll**

You, yourself, as much as anybody in the entire universe, deserve your love and affection.
—**Buddha**

Acceptance

I am a mother, wife, sister, daughter and friend. I am a writer and actor. I am thoughtful, empathic and creative. I am wise, witty and funny.

I am not OCD.

Yes, I have mastered OCD. Although it is a disorder that may never be cured, I have a choice to wallow in self-pity or claim inner pride; I have a choice to fall victim to my rituals or to sit with fear until it subsides. We all have this choice. We all possess the free will to perceive the glass as half empty or half full.

Part of our road to recovery with OCD is accepting we have the disorder, yet simultaneously realizing we *are not* the disorder any more than cancer or any other disease *is* a person. You are a multi-faceted human being who is capable of achieving greatness, who just happens to have OCD. Don't let your greatness be eclipsed by a disorder. OCD is no different than impulsivity or a shy disposition: it just *is* the way your brain is wired. You may be born that way, but you can change it. Don't beat yourself up because of a misfiring in your brain any more than you would beat yourself up for having diabetes. It's a waste of energy. Instead, put your energy into moving forward with grace and equanimity, toward a life of freedom from OCD.

Acceptance

Sheri talks about accepting and not allowing her OCD to define her. This is a powerful realization and one that can help sufferers begin to take back their lives. As with facing any adversity in life, whether it is disease, addiction, divorce or the death of a loved one, we must first accept the situation is indeed present before we can make movement toward change. In looking at the grief model (and accepting that OCD exists in your life involves grieving), denial or disbelief is a common first reaction. Consequently, people tend to initially deny OCD is a problem for them. Compounded with the irrational, underlying belief OCD is somehow helpful can make the denial even more compelling. **Accepting OCD does not mean you like it or you would choose it or you are "giving up." It simply involves calling it what it is.**

If you suffer with OCD, it may be advantageous for you to make a list of all of the ways that OCD interferes with your life. In therapy, sometime in the first few sessions, I have clients make a list of the ways their rituals and avoidances negatively impact their lives. This ultimately leads to "what would my life be like if I did not have OCD?" Helping people to identify the negative consequences of their behavior can move them into acceptance and, ultimately, readiness for change. Go ahead, take a piece of paper and write down all of the ways OCD interferes:

- Do your rituals, compulsions, avoidances and obsessions take up more than one hour each day?
- Do any of your OCD behaviors keep you from interacting with certain people, from going to certain places, from touching certain things?
- Do OCD behaviors prevent you from having close relationships?
- Do OCD behaviors cause you problems in your work life?

If the answer is "yes" to any of these questions, then maybe it is time to take a step forward, a step toward treatment. Acceptance requires you admit OCD is a problem *and* you are willing to make the necessary sacrifices to improve your life. Once you are here, your options for the future open up significantly.

Another important part of the acceptance process is dealing with feelings of shame. Shame is an insidious emotion that, left unrecognized, has the potential to create unforeseen roadblocks in the treatment process. Sometimes people with psychological issues, e.g., depression, anxiety, OCD, are ashamed they have the problem and, more importantly, are ashamed they cannot "solve" the problem on their own. For some reason, disorders of the mind carry with them an assumption they "should" be dealt with "in the mind" by thinking or willing them away. This is why taking psychotropic medications is often difficult for some people. Unfortunately, "solving" OCD by oneself is next to impossible. As Sheri describes just above, accepting OCD *just is*, is a key to moving forward. Remember not to judge yourself for having OCD, for not being able to eradicate it on your own and for the negative impact on your life. True acceptance is a loving and compassionate process where you are willing to look at yourself, warts and all, and to embrace all aspects of you. OCD is just that, one aspect of your beautiful, complicated self.

Be Active in Your Recovery

ERP treatment for OCD is quite effective, but you have to *do* it. It requires a willingness to participate actively, to take risks and to feel somewhat uncomfortable. Unfortunately, one in four people refuse to do ERP precisely because of these requirements. Sometimes clients report to me, "I tried ERP and it didn't work." Upon further questioning, I learn that either they were not participating in ERP, due to therapist error (either being poorly trained or unfamiliar with the concepts of ERP), or the client did not *actively* participate in therapy. ERP treatment DOES work, quite well in fact. But it requires your active involvement and persistence. Ask yourself:

- Am I ready to actively participate in therapy?
- Am I ready to take some risks?
- Have I identified a trained professional who has experience treating people with OCD using ERP; am I willing to trust the process and take some risks?

Climb up on some hill at sunrise. Everybody needs perspective once in a while, and you'll find it there.

—Robb Sagendorph

The best way to find yourself is to lose yourself in the service of others.

—Mahatma Gandhi

A Shift in Perspective

Whenever I feel a nagging pull to check something, I force myself to imagine how I would explain my odd behavior to our children. *What would my kids say if they could see me jump in and out of the bed a dozen times to stare at our front door? How would they look at me if they caught me opening and closing the door to my office over and over?* When I consider the possibility they could discover their mother behaving irrationally, a rush of shame floods my veins and suddenly I find myself more determined than ever to sit with my pulls.

Regardless of your fears, and your pulls to check and ritualize, a key motivator for keeping OCD from recurring is to know what motivates you in the first place. News anchor (KCBS Radio in San Francisco) and spokesman for the nonprofit International OCD Foundation, Jeff Bell (author of *When in Doubt, Make Belief*) offers OCD sufferers what he refers to as The Greater Good Perspective Shift. In the example of my sons' walking in on me mid-compulsion, Bell's theory would suggest I consider the negative ramifications of performing my rituals and compulsions in front of the two of them. The Greater Good in this case would be to sit with my pulls, knowing I am modeling for my children a confident, healthy mother who doesn't acquiesce to her fears.

Maybe you want to work at a particular store, but are terrified at the idea of needing to shake strangers' hands. Perhaps you want to babysit your newborn nephew, but cannot stop obsessing over the idea you might cause him bodily harm. Again, it doesn't matter what your fears are; what matters is you address those fears and face them to attain the Greater Good (e.g., working at your favorite store or spending time with your nephew). And Bell's Greater Good Perspective Shift is a potent tool for change and preventing our fears from taking over in the future.

When we focus on the "big picture" (e.g. our loved ones, family members, our community, our career plans, etc.) we are able to clearly see what is important to us. By shifting perspective, we suddenly remember there is a whole world out there for us to enjoy and care about. When we think of others more than ourselves, we are helping to prevent OCD from returning and by extension, living a life of true freedom.

Writing this book with Suzanne has been my own source of Greater Good. When we first began this manuscript, I no longer had clinically diagnosable OCD and was down to about five minutes of rituals and compulsions per day. I am happy to report I am now down to barely two minutes—all thanks to you, the reader! YOU are one major reason I push myself to sit with pulls. Knowing you are reading this book in hopes of understanding yourself and your OCD, as well as learning some helpful tools for mastering OCD, gives me strength to keep challenging myself because it keeps me accountable. Now when I feel a pull to check something, I not only consider our children, but more and more I think of you as well. Each time I sit with a pull and conquer it I think, *"Yes—I sat through my anxiety for you (the reader) and did it (for all of us)!!!"*

Take a moment to consider who in your life motivates you to sit with your anxiety so that you no longer fear it. It doesn't have to be a person. Maybe it's your career. Maybe it's an activity you've always wanted to do but have been too terrified to attempt because of OCD's warnings. Maybe it's a trip or something you've needed or wanted to take. Find out what OCD is preventing you from doing and look at the Greater Good, the amazing benefits (freedom!) you will reap from regularly challenging OCD.

The other day I told Suzanne I only had a few rituals left.

"That is great! I am curious though, if you were a cancer patient and the surgeon offered to take out either ninety-five percent or one hundred percent of the malignancy, which option would you prefer?" she asked.

"One hundred percent," I gulped.

"Exactly. Now Sheri, you know if you allow some rituals to remain and 'deem' them okay, you leave a window open for OCD to return."

I am now down to even less than when we spoke. In fact, for the past couple of nights, I have only checked two things. It was HARD work to get to this point, but I notice the more I challenge myself, the easier it is to keep going. And while the whisper to check remains, I'm getting better at ignoring it. Knowing my own personal Greater Good (my children, my husband, everyone out there who wants to master OCD) pushes me onward!

You deserve a life of freedom. The pain of sitting through the desire to check, touch, pray, etc. might feel unbearable, but it does diminish and in its place comes confidence, flexibility and tolerance for doubt. OCD only gives you more fear, imposing you in a self-created prison. Regularly challenging OCD allows you to function fully in this world where you can help others. **No benefit ever came from following OCD's demands.** Freedom is a benefit worth fighting for.

I always wanted a happy ending... Now I've learned, the hard way, that some poems don't rhyme, and some stories don't have a clear beginning, middle and end. Life is about not knowing, having to change, taking the moment and making the best of it without knowing what's going to happen next. Delicious ambiguity.

—**Gilda Radner**

Climbing Out of the Rabbit Hole

Now the ball is in your court. Sheri and I have, I hope, sketched a picture for you, illustrating the development of moderate OCD in a young woman's life, the events that may have colored her OCD picture and her vibrant path to recovery. She has courageously disclosed her traumatic history, and her secret life down the rabbit hole with OCD. She has claimed her weaknesses, divulged her vulnerabilities and has beautifully articulated the difficult, but doable journey into recovery.

Interestingly, it was not until this book was in the editing stage that I realized the incredible parallel process Sheri had in her life: her break with her toxic family paralleling her break with OCD. Maybe Sheri's realizing her parents' negative messages and abusive commands were unacceptable later helped her to see her OCD, too, was unacceptable. Like Alice standing up to the Queen of Hearts, maybe standing up to her dysfunctional parents ultimately helped Sheri stand up to and resist the demands of her OCD. We will never know for sure, but in the end, you can learn from Sheri and her journey out of the prison of OCD.

I chose to be a part of this project because I wanted to help Sheri tell her story, as it is worth telling. In psychology books, too often the personal and "real" side of the clinical story is not told. Many self-help books focus on "what to do" and forget to tell "how I did it!" Well, Sheri did it and she did it well.

I hope reading this book has been helpful to you from both a personal and a psychological perspective. I hope you walk away with encouragement, motivation and a clearer understanding of what the road ahead might look like. Most importantly, I hope you feel understood. Although each person with OCD suffers in a unique way, the suffering is universal. Of all the many psychological disorders I have treated in the past several decades, treating people with OCD is one of the most rewarding. It is an honor to help people to feel understood, not misunderstood; validated, not judged; and, liberated, not confined to a self-contained prison cell.

The door to your prison cell is open. Go ahead and walk out into the freedom of the world without complicated rules and rituals. Yes, there may be danger out there, there may be risks and complications along the way, but there is also boundless freedom. Although it may feel risky to leave the "safety" of your OCD, remember there are risks inside your prison cell as well: the risk of missing out on life, the risk of not enjoying people who are close to you, the risk of isolation from your world. You cannot ever permanently ensure your safety and the safety of the ones you love inside your prison cell; you can only ensure your suffering. Go ahead, walk through the door that was and is always open to you: the door to freedom.

Bibliography

American Psychiatric Association. *Diagnostic and Statistical Manual of Mental Disorders.* 4th ed. Washington, D.C.: Author, 1994.

Baer, Lee. (2012). *Getting Control: Overcoming Your Obsessions and Compulsions.* New York, NY: Penguin.

Bejerot, Nils (1974). The six day war in Stockholm. New Scientist, volume 61, number 886, page 486-487.

Bassett, Lucinda. (1996). *From Panic to Power.* New York, NY: Harper Collins Publishers

Bell, Jeff. (2009) *When in Doubt, Make Belief : An OCD-Inspired Approach to Living with Uncertainty.* Novato, CA: New World Library Location.

C., Roy. (1999). *Obsessive Compulsive Disorder: A Survival Guide For Family And Friends.* New Hyde Park, NY: Obsessive Compulsive Anonymous World Services, Inc.

Carroll, Lewis (1865). *Alice's Adventures in Wonderland.* New York, NY: Macmillan Publishers.

Garlin, Jeff. (2010). *My Footprint: Carrying the Weight of the World.* New York, NY: Gallery Books, a Division of Simon and Shuster.

Gius, Mary. (2006). *Living With Severe Obsessive Compulsive Disorder.* Bothell, WA: Book Publishers Network.

Gravitz, Herbert. (2004). *Obsessive Compulsive Disorder: New Help for the Family.* Holt, MI: Partners Publishers Group.

Grayson, Jonathan. (2004). *Freedom From Obsessive-Compulsive Disorder: A Personalized Recovery Program for Living with Uncertainty.* New York, NY: Berkley Trade.

Hay, Louise. (1999) *You Can Heal Your Life.* Carlsbad. CA: Hay House Inc.

King, Stephen (1977). *The Shining.* New York, NY: Doubleday.

Landsman, Karen. (2005). *Loving Someone with OCD: Help for You and Your Family.* Oakland, CA: New Harbinger Publications.

Mackenzie, Ian K. (2004). The Stockholm Syndrome Revisited: Hostages, Relationships, Prediction, Control and Psychological Science". *Journal of Police Crisis Negotiations,* 4(1): 5-21.

Penzel, Fred. *Obsessive-Compulsive Disorders: A Complete Guide to Getting Well and Staying Well.* New York, NY: Oxford University Press.

Rowling, J.K., (1999) *The Prisoner of Azkaban.* Broadway, NY: Scholastic Inc.

The Shining. Directed by Stanley Kubrick. 1980.

The Aviator. Directed by Martin Scorsese. 2004.

A Beautiful Mind. Directed by Ron Howard. 2001.

Curb Your Enthusiasm. Directed by Robert B. Weide. 2000.

What the BLEEP Do We Know? (documentary) Film first released in 2004 Captured Light Industries; A Lord of the Wind Film Co-Writers: William Arntz, Betsy Chasse, Mark Vicente. Filmed in Portland, OR.

.